GREAT
memories

BY JJ BRENNEMAN

Great Memories

Trilogy Christian Publishers A Wholly Owned Subsidiary of Trinity Broadcasting Network

2442 Michelle Drive Tustin, CA 92780

Rights Department, 2442 Michelle Drive, Tustin, CA 92780.

Trilogy Christian Publishing/TBN and colophon are trademarks of Trinity Broadcasting Network.

For information about special discounts for bulk purchases, please contact Trilogy Christian Publishing.

Manufactured in the United States of America

10 9 8 7 6 5 4 3 2 1

Library of Congress Cataloging-in-Publication Data is available.

ISBN: 979-8-88738-071-1

E-ISBN: 979-8-88738-072-8

DEDICATION

To my loving and sweetest-ever parents, gorgeous Nancy Jo, my best-ever friends Larry and Jane, Michael and Victoria, Miss T, my wise disciples Mike and Bernice, my sister, Rida, and my most precious, loving, smart-as-a-whip, and adorable son, Owen. Y'all make me happy, loved, and completely fulfilled.

And to my Owen: you're pure, heaven-sent *magic* to me, and you'll always be the very *best* of me and your mom.

CONTENTS

FOREWORD

It's my prayer these stories (or even one) grab your attention and hit you in your present season (maybe exactly when you need it from Him). If just one person sees themselves somewhere in these pages, I hope it helps you get through whatever obstacles are blocking you from getting to your best days...and/or makes it easier to get through them too.

God gifted me with a moral compass, a discerning mind, and the skill of writing so you may, somehow, *feel* my stories. I don't do that intentionally; it's by His direction. I only choose to comply, and I'm so blessed to oblige Him. Doing that gives me the greatest, safest peace I've ever known, the direction He has shown me, and the happiness of sharing His *good news*.

I hope some of these stories make you laugh, smile, and/or think. And furthermore, I hope they cast light on what your life would be like with God in it; He certainly changed my life when I gave Him *all* of me. You can be free, too. God bless you.

INTRODUCTION

Most of these stories have been with me for a very long time and have been refined over time (because they were not ready yet). I hope you enjoy the variety of these stories, but I must tell you I only write a story when it really moves me into putting it down on paper because of all the emotional significance surrounding it.

I have a mix of stories: some have religious themes; four or five of them are all about my goofy son growing up; there are children's stories (some from actual events), and there are stories about things I've experienced and learned on my fortunate travels.

Blessedly, I was resoundingly happy to have a dad who told me (when I was very young), "You need to go out and make your own memories. You're not going to make any sitting around here." He added, "Then, you'll have some very interesting stories to tell."

And I do!

My dad was an over-the-road trucker for over six years and was in lots of places, mostly by himself, and experienced the most scenic places out West. Once, he took me to California when I was only twelve years old for me to see more of my family.

On the way, I was standing in the middle of a desert with competing skies (thunderstorms and rainbows) all around me, and my dad said I was holding lava.

"Lava, really, Dad?" I also said, "It's only rocks and dirt, but this is the most beautiful thing I've ever seen."

It was the first time (of many) my dad alerted me, "Now, that's profound, son."

Dad also taught me to thoroughly enjoy the little things. I learned from him to appreciate everything: "Always keep looking around. You never know what you'll miss. It might be the only time you'll ever see it."

He and I were once twelve miles from the Grand Canyon, and my dad realized my mother's birthday was two days away. He cringed when he told me, "We're gonna miss it this time, buddy. But we'll be back here someday."

Seventeen years later, my wife and I finally saw the pristine, breathtaking awe of the Grand Canyon at near sunset. Some things, I suppose, just take a little while to age. That's how I explain these stories.

Please, *please* enjoy them, and I also hope you see yourselves in some of them!

GERTRUDE'S BIG ICE-CREAM CONE

It was a hot, sticky afternoon on the Kansas plains. Humidity aside, it didn't affect Gertrude because she was smiling ear to ear. She proudly fluffed her white feathers all over because, this morning, Farmer John announced she was the new Head Hen.

"All right, ladies," she cackled. "Let's start laying some eggs. We don't want Farmer John mad at us."

Gertrude wasn't worried, though; her hens were egg-laying machines. And she secretly thought, *My sweet chickadees can lay a hundred eggs anytime I want!*

Gertrude tiptoed over to the bunkhouse to see how her human kids were doing. But she didn't see Penny or Tony. However, something ominous in the sky quickly caught her eye; it looked exactly like one of Penny's huge waffle ice-cream cones dripping all over with vanilla ice cream and her other favorite delight, mousse chocolate. But this cone was oversized.

It was also grey, black, and white, with jagged bolts of lightning crashing all inside its swirling clouds. Gertrude told herself, "It seems a lot more like one of Tony's spinning tops." But this cone was getting closer and closer. Puzzled, she thought, *That's weird*, and wondered, *Why is an ice-cream cone up in the sky anyway?*

Before she knew it, the huge ice-cream cone smashed down on the ground with a thunderous thud. Gertrude's eyes bulged when she first saw it hit Farmer John's tractor and then throw it into their neighbor's house. They were both smashed to bits, and she heard a ferocious whooshing sound!

When she didn't see the ice-cream cone stop, Gertrude got up on a few stacked bales of hay and yelled out to her hens, "Watch out, ladies; it's coming right for us!" Then, Gertrude turned and blew her trusty Head-Hen whistle with everything she could muster, warning her hens to quickly line up inside the henhouse. But she also had to look out for her other friends and get them out of danger!

Next, she hurriedly pushed on the door, but it would not budge. Panic set in, and with an emotionally wretched voice, she squawked, "Oh, no. The door's locked!" She reminded her frightened hens, "Remember when Farmer John bolted the door to keep those big bad wolves from getting to us?"

Gertrude's friend, Metilda, chirped, "Now, what should we do, Gertrude? If you don't do something, we're all going to die." That was when Gertrude bent down to hide her eyes; she didn't want her girls to see how petrified she was for all of them. For just the briefest of seconds, she let herself fearfully predict, *We're probably all goners!*

But then, Gertrude looked out of her Head-Hen window and was relieved to see Old Rusty (the trusted ol' family hound) sniffing around for food. She blew hard on her trusty silver whistle, and Rusty ran right over, barking. He said, "Why did you do that so loud, Gertrude? You're gonna hurt my tender ears."

Gertrude shot back, "You gotta come break us out, Rusty. Look behind you at that enormous ice-cream cone!"

As the old beagle turned around, he saw the sheer magnitude of it and yipped, "Oh, gosh!" and rubbed his paws over his nose. After a second of reasoning, he gruffed, "I'll go chase down Penny. She'll be able to break everybody out!"

But when Old Rusty started to run, a giant lightning bolt crashed into the ground behind them. All Gertrude heard was a deafening crack! And, for a split second, everyone was blinded by the severely bright light. After all that, they saw a gigantic crater right near the back of their henhouse. And, unfortunately, the latter was on fire!

That was when Gertrude grabbed the command reins and immediately took charge. She yelled, "Run through that hole and head for the big barn, everybody!" And, just then, Penny, Tony, Brunhilda the cat, and Old Rusty came rushing over. Gertrude was fast-tracking all her hens up to the big barn, so they just followed Gertrude's lead.

Farmer John ventured out to see Gertrude and everyone flying right by him and into the big barn. Gertrude picked up the big man's concern when he loudly shot out, "What's all the fuss about, Gerty?"

But all a weakened Gertrude could voice was, "Look up there, Farmer John, at that big ice-cream cone coming straight for the farm and us!"

Gertrude watched Farmer John look past the crowd and in the general direction of his burning henhouse. Then, his skin turned ash grey, and she could tell he was very afraid. The only thing she heard him next say was, "That's no ice-cream cone, Gerty! That's a twister tornado!"

Gertrude barely heard how, once he gathered himself, Farmer John screamed, "Y'all get down in the big barn's cellar right now! I'll run and get Mama, and very quickly, we'll both meet you down there."

Likewise, Gertrude ordered her chicks down into the big barn's deep, dark, underground storm cellar.

Several seconds passed, and Gertrude was moving over to let Farmer John and his wife drop down into the cellar with almost every other scared member of their farm family.

A hush came over everyone as they all sat fiercely still and silent. The "quarters" were very cramped, and Gertrude was squatting with everyone else and listening to the giant ice-cream cone pass over their heads. After it went by, Betty Jo quacked, "It sounded just like a full-blown choo choo train."

After it was finally over, Gertrude was the last one to climb out of the dimly lit cellar. That was when she witnessed 360 degrees of devastation! The animals that didn't make it down the cellar were all wobbly, hobbling around, or shell-shocked. She also glanced over to catch Farmer John's family holding each other and quietly crying.

But in a few quiet seconds, Gertrude could feel Farmer John lean his big frame down until he was almost even with her. That was when she saw the huge man's eyes were still wet. But Gertrude was more confused when she saw a big smile appear through his fresh tears.

Very meekly, she asked him, "How can you be you smiling, Farmer John? That great big ice-cream cone crashed down on our nice, quaint farm and blew everything away! How can you possibly be close to okay about all this?"

That was when Farmer John's newly crowned Head Hen felt a whiskered kiss brush over her shivering beak.

His whisper of an answer rang over her tiny eardrum, "It's okay, Gertrude! Everything's gonna be fine! That's because you saved everybody, Missy. Thank you, my sweet-sweet, little Mother Hen!"

ICE-CREAM BALLS

My dad died earlier this year, and I'm just starting to come to grips with everything about him and me.

I slowly realize how much it hurts knowing I'll never see or talk to him again. And I'll never hear his voice again, even though he seemed as if he'd live forever. My dad always wanted to be older than his dad when he died (forty-seven years old), and he made it to seventy-seven years old.

Worse than losing him is the shock that's still there; I'm probably shocked because I've never let myself really break down and cry over losing him. Not doing it probably means he was very important to me and it'll hurt very badly.

Maybe I'll never really lose him. But, right now, I just can't break down and cry about losing my dad. When he died, I seemed to constantly be in "playback mode" (reliving all my best memories with him and recounting all the lessons he gifted me with about life).

My dad was always there for everyone he loved! He did everything a father is supposed to do, and I'll always appreciate every lesson he taught me; many of them saved me. Sadly, I don't believe a lot of people appreciate many things. But Dad always taught me to appreciate everything, and I do. It also feels good to treasure "the little things," as he mused.

Even now, I really can't cry. But I remember the last time we talked. He was frustrated with the lousy care he was getting for a diabolical lung condition. But I didn't know he was close to his last days. It might be why he emailed us right before Christmas; his apology was his last present to us. But it was not warranted. And every Christmas, I'll reread it.

He recounted some of his regrets, but I've long since thought he had no reason to apologize and/or ask us for our forgiveness. I forgave my dad (and myself) a long time ago. We were both stubborn and selfish, and I'm honored my son was around him a few great times. My dad was always there for us in his own, extremely special, Joe-like way!

I call the time when my son and I visited my dad "completing a miraculous circle of life." His son now had a son, and we were all, finally, together! It was one of the happiest weeks of my life (enough "to beat the band"), and there were oodles of love inside all of us. Obviously, I wanted more time, but this was enough quality time; I appreciated it for exactly what it was. But I've spent so many years wanting more but not enough years appreciating what I did have (which was quite a lot and more than most kids got).

Maybe I failed at appreciating everything, but I learned my dad's lessons well (and I pass them on to his grandson). If I had one wish in my life, it'd be for my son to be around my dad a lot more. My father was a great dad to six sons, and he had always been there for every one of us.

He taught me about the value of money when I was around six years old. I was working very soon after and, finally, getting things I wanted (and trying to be what Dad called "magnanimous" wherever I could). We didn't have much, so I was immaturely jealous of others; I blamed them for having so much more than me. But sometimes I was furious because they didn't seem to appreciate anything! I remember a schoolmate having a brand-new car (I had never had one), then smashing it to bits. The next day he had a new one. What?

But learning Dad's monetary lessons taught me to earn my own things. Pretty soon, I also realized the only way I was going to have anything was by earning it. I earned a lot, and Dad's lessons are carrying me through the rest of my life just as he wanted.

When I was a young lad earning my own wage in the summers, the Good Humor ice-cream truck drove up and down our busy street nearly every summer day. The weirdest song continuously bellowed from the little blue truck, tempting all my friends and me to come (like some "Pied Piper"). Luckily, I had some coin in my pocket when I wanted some ice cream.

When I was about ten years old, my dad was an over-the-road truck driver; he was away fourteen to sixteen days a trip. And even when he got back, he was only home for a very short week. My family accepted it like the hazy, hot, and humid days we suffered in Philly. We didn't really have a choice. As the saying goes, "it is what it is" (and it never ever, unfortunately, changed).

Likewise, when the Good Humor man zoomed around our mazelike neighborhood, I always felt magnanimous toward my dad and whichever brothers were around. It felt amazing to treat my family with the money I earned. And it was thrilling for me to do something nice for my mom when we normally didn't have much. I called it, "An unexpected bonus, Mom!"

Fortunately, one gift was to show my dad the gratitude and adoration I felt for him for so many things he did for me—my whole life, all ten years! So, when he was finally home, my dad really liked a pint of chocolate ice cream. *Dad's*, I thought, *old-fashioned.* But I required a pint of mint chocolate-chip ice cream (with a little cooler zing to my tasty ice-cream treat).

Many days I thought about buying my dad a pint of his favorite ice cream. There are many cherished memories between my dad and me, but those ice-cream days were special. We'd sit and talk about lots of things, and once again, Dad would teach me a unique way to eat pints.

You had to use a small spoon.

"You'll only eat a little bit of ice cream every time," he advised. "The trick is scooping away ice cream from every side and down to the bottom." Finishing, he'd state, "All that's left is a small, even tastier ball of ice cream, sitting right at the bottom."

The smaller spoonfuls were delicious only because Dad taught me about appreciating little things in life. I learned to appreciate the smallest facets of things, including listening to (crazily loud) Pink Floyd's *Dark Side of the Moon* when my stepmom couldn't stand hearing it. And I really loved spooning my way to the bottom of my pint to get to my little ball of ice cream. I didn't know there was also going to be a wonderful, lasting memory at the bottom of every pint with my dad!

That small ball of ice cream was a quintessential, flavor-empowered bonanza! And I will never know that same feeling without my dad; it wasn't just the ice cream tasting sweet; my dad embodied sweetness and true, unconditional love. To me, he was my real treat! Nowadays, when I pass a cooler of a variety of delicious flavors of ice cream, I smile. I realized my dad gave me many different pints all my life. Thanks, Dad!

I earned ice-cream money; I've been able to be "magnanimous" with lots of people I love and was, most importantly, extremely loved by a man I'll forever adore (and miss terribly).

I always loved being around my dad, learning lots of things like being able to stand on my two feet and fighting back at the "big bad world"; Dad even taught me, "The world can really be bad, so always be cautious." It was about being aware but also living fearlessly!

My dad always made my life fun and made it easier for me to navigate troubled waters because I was always able to go to him. He also taught me how to survive and how to tenderly appreciate life's simplest things; he trained me up to feel all life had to offer me. Mostly, he wanted me to be as happy as I could, and it's the same wish I have for my son. Genetics?

Part of my gratitude is loving pints of ice cream right down to the yummy, teeny-tiny ice-cream ball! I know I'll never have another pint with Pop, but that's all right. Maybe, someday, I'll have a pint and finally cry over missing him. But anyway, he'll never really leave me. Daddy-O, my ice cream ball was outrageously tasty because of only you.

PS

My dad never told me what *life* meant. But he taught me enough about "the big picture" for me to derive my own meaning: "Living In the Fullness of your Experiences" (he said, "You must make your own memories").

BOOM

Daydreaming:

What did Joey tell me? "If you see." Oh, yeah. If I see the car's red (brake) lights, it means this guy's backing up and is thoroughly determined to chase us all down for our "crimes against humanity" (and his shell-shocked car). And notice: I should scream bloody murder to my comrades, "Red lights, red lights, red lights!"

Likewise, his brake lights flash, and I snap out of my daydream and yell as if our lives depend on it.

But this is crazy nuts, and it's all a mess now. Seconds ago, we were celebrating another crushing victory. Granted, our day began radically cool, too.

The sky was a crystal-clear blue, and the air was amazingly fresh (a balmy twenty-six degrees). That made the snow crunch under our flimsy boots. The snow was perfect; it had to have the right combination of reasonable cold and a smidgeon of moisture. My little brother liked it because it was "jammin' for making abominable snowmen." It also made packing fist-sized snowballs easier, enabling us to throw big ones that perfectly fit our hands.

The right mix of moisture kept us from throwing ice balls. The unspoken rule in our neighborhood was: "Never throw ice balls!" They break car windows, and Joey always told us, "No one needs that hassle." All we wanted was good, clean fun!

Our leaders, Joey (eighteen years old) and his baby brother, Jimmy (seventeen), were steadily barking out orders to us. Joey proudly told me, "Jimmy, you have the best arm, so go hide near the school until I give you the signal!"

My buddies, meanwhile, huddled together, stealthily quiet, behind the snow wall we strategically built on the precipice of Whitehall Lane. From above, the street looked like a very long, dog-right semicircle hiding in Northeast Philly's burbs. Whitehall merged with Sussex, and it sloped down to Morrell Avenue (our main thoroughfare). In fact, our neighborhood was named Morrell Park (after some rich benefactor who donated his farm in his will).

Whitehall Lane was barely passable, straddled on both sides by hulky '60s cars. But it was our concrete playground, and we called our fort "Headquarters." I wore a Cheshire grin and reminisced about all the silly made-up games we played in our imaginary "jungle."

Grown-ups called our neighborhood "the Maze": every street ran into a bigger-semicircle avenue (and every street was back-to-back with another house on another semicircle street). We weren't concerned. We were too busy doin' our own thing. And it was extra "neat" that our new school and my playground sat within shouting distance of each other. Even my dad once observed, "Whoever drew this up was really smart and practical."

Our small houses were tightly bunched together, like sardines, and years later, I noticed they were smaller. I wondered, "How had everyone fit in there?" Despite its stature, our street was chock-full of a zillion of kids of all colors, shapes, and sizes (all a city kid ever wanted).

The moms always needed a break, and they'd say, "Go out 'n' play!" (which was not neglectful because every driver knew: "Keep your eyes peeled out for kids"). And my mom always begged us, "Wud'ja get out in the fresh air already?" (pleading, "Leave me alone for one blessed second"). Other moms screamed, "Make up your minds! Either in or out" (because we always ran in and out of each other's homes). Maybe we were just indecisive?

My mom loved saying, "Am I cooling the outside, too?" But the concept was lost on me. We didn't have AC units, so working fans were pure nighttime blessings; we were drenched in sweat and prayed for a cool breeze to come our way. When it did, it was pure heaven!

Winters were much different: we loved having army-like territorial snowball fights all day long. By noon, we had already pounded each other for the 949th time. So, for a nice change of pace, we directed our energies toward making a few more drivers' lives full of unbearable agony. "When you pass by our corner," we'd justify, "the crashing snowballs are your convenience toll."

My buddies and I lined up a half dozen fist-sized snow-balls on the wall of our frozen fortress overlooking Sussex Lane. And our youngest rebel, Michael Titano, was scouting across the wider street. "Your only job," Joey said, "is to watch out for the next car." Before the next car neared us, Mikey would scream, "Get ready, guys!" Then, Joey commanded us, "Wait till the next car gets within range. Then, let 'em have it!"

Fortunately, Sussex Lane's speed limit was a slow 25 mph. And when the next car crawled forward, we launched 1,000 volleys right at their ill-fated vehicle.

On the hilly portion in front of us, drivers were also worried they'd slide down to Morrell Avenue way too fast. Consequently, they'd slow down to 10–15 mph. Realizing our melee would, happily, last longer made us seriously lose our minds! *Sorry, drivers. We're just having fun!*

We pelted those unfortunate cars beyond belief. Shell-shocked drivers crawled out of their pimpled cars and spent hysterical moments trying to find "those menacing kids." Despite that, in wintertime, in our Maze, our special brand of mischief was commonplace. Given that startling reality, our tumultuous onslaught was often discouraging and debilitating.

Halfheartedly, they'd try to chase us, but concession came quickly. We didn't want to hurt anyone, but our good times were not possible without their assistance. I thought, *If the drivers only knew we could have hammered them with ice balls.* It reminded me of the times when, instead of my dad consoling me, he'd say, "I could really give you something to cry about." Huh?

The hilarious part was the drivers never knew the shelling was not over; prematurely, they realized, *Oh. The danger's over.* But little did they know there was so much more fun coming their way very soon!

Joey placed me at the school because of my great arm. He knew I was a Little League center fielder, and I loved throwing out base runners. I loved my dad, and he called it "rocketing a ball on a clothesline," thereby zinging supersonic throws to our catcher (mostly to the dismay of another astonished, teary-eyed base runner). You're out!

I waited patiently for the signal; Joey said he'd yell, "Get ready, Jim," right after we pelted the next unlucky car with a zillion vicious snowballs. I laughed, hearing the snowballs pummeling each car's fresh steel like machine guns blasting away, "Rat-a-tat-tat, blammity-blam-blam, blammity-blammmm-*bammmm*!" Fortunately, the sound was nothing compared to the earth-shattering deluge each petrified driver was painstakingly enduring.

Meanwhile, all the noisy ruckuses made me miss Joey's signal! When the artillery ceased and my target busily swerved down Sussex, I heard Joey call out; he ordered, "Wait till the car gets near Morrell!" By then, we knew each driver was operating under a false sense of security. And I realized he was clueless about round two!

Once the car was in the right target area, Joey ordered, "Launch that huge snowball, Jimmy!" And while my boomer was raining down on the car, I thought, *This guy doesn't know anything about his next few moments!* I was almost mercilessly sorry about the sheer trauma my towering snowball was about to unleash on his innocent life.

I've always had an accurate aim, and at that ominous hour, my ferocious snowball rocketed back down and headed straight for this unsuspecting guy's roof. After scouring the heavens, my huge, fully packed snowball crashed down on top of its intended prey!

The beauty of a '60s car is their roofs are almost entirely made of steel. Naturally, when my heavily loaded snowball crashed into his roof, the reverberating *boom* was "screechingly" loud! The noise was monstrous and echoed around the Maze (and even people inside their homes came out to see: "What's the fuss all about?").

The freaked-out driver was swerving, "All over kingdom come," and I laughed uncontrollably. But I did sympathize with him, thinking, *It must be sheer chaotic terror inside that car!*

Once the thundering boom ended, I knew he was gonna be so mad and bent on revenge. Still, as crazy as it sounds, I heard my mom (skilled at stating the obvious) say, "He'll certainly be fit to be tied!" Really, Mom? Seconds after this latest realization, I kept on chuckling, but I stammered, "Oh no! There are those red lights Joey warned me about!"

Joey schooled me, "Remember, Jimmy? When you see red lights, you gotta tell everybody, 'Run!' It means the driver's super mad! So, warn everybody, Jimmy!"

I felt compelled, so I promised him, "You can trust me, Joey."

Likewise, when I saw the red lights, I yelled out as loud as I could, "Run, you guys; he's coming back!" But I was still super giddy, though, if I had any sense, I should have surmised I'd be the first munchkin he'd come for. But I was hoping he wouldn't find out where I launched my rain of terror.

After screaming my warning, I sank down behind the wall and stayed eerily quiet. They named my school "John Hancock" after a very heroic man who was brave enough to sign his name (in really huge letters) on a very important American document. Supposedly, my wickedly sounding snowball was also a convincing signature on that driver's roof!

When I guessed it was safe, I peeked out. When I saw him getting out of his car, it was painfully obvious the sudden near-death experience clearly rattled his cage. And after not catching us right away, he shook his fist and lamented, "What can I do now?"

Then, he got back into his car, thinking, *Those evil monsters are long gone*. But it didn't console him. Suddenly, though, he looked toward my hiding spot and screamed, "If I ever catch you, little pip-squeak, I'm gonna pound you as you just pounded my roof!" Talk about scary!

Whew-wee! The whole drama frazzled me, but I just couldn't stop giggling. This guy was making it impossible to stop, and he couldn't find me without my comrades. I knew they were all safe at home, so I reckoned, *It's smarter to simply hide out here just a wee bit longer!*

Afterward, the den of mischief-makers gathered in Joey's house for celebratory cheesesteaks. My boys all raved about my massively booming snowball and how petrified they were, running away. And we agreed, "He'd never catch us anyway." But the adrenaline-fueled panic was crazy, and we instinctively knew it'd never get better than this!

Nowadays, with a perfect snow mix, I hear Joey say, "Launch another booming snowball" (and watch it plummet down on another naïve mark). As grown-ups, we're told, "Put away childish things." However, the memories of my "little troublemaker" days are crazy fun to remember.

Somehow, I sympathetically hoped all the drivers' roofs we crashed also launched some massive snowballs on high! I still hear echoes of those ear-splitting booms hitting every rooftop. And I still laugh myself silly because they were so much louder in that cool morning air.

Nowadays, in wintertime, whenever I'm driving around the fun neighborhood that raised me, I still look out for hooligans. Once, I was pelted pretty well by some fun-loving, overly rambunctious youths. But their assaults were impish shellings compared to the all-out blammity-blamm-blamm-boom pounding we gave people on White-hall Lane. I laugh about it now and think, *It was good ol' winter fun* (a "passing of the torch"). But it was also some of my favorite times! For me, wintertime will always be crazy cold and full of laughs!

Right then, I got out of my car to look for any young whippersnappers preparing to trounce it. I pondered, *Is there an older kid out there with the best arm waiting to pound my roof with his killer-loud boom? Not now, I demand! But I must confess: I deserve it. But I'd rather it was somebody else's roof!*

I hope I'll never endure one of my prototype boomers because it wouldn't be much fun living through that bombardment. It's a deafening roar of concussive booming when it finally screams down on your little car's roof, filling your ears with a super-frightening, life-altering, shell-shocking, trauma-inducing crash!

Here's to extremely fun winters! I hope they all include fist-packed, moist-enough snowballs (and a few crazy-loud booms)—that's only if you're terribly deserving or extremely unlucky. It's anyone's guess: Who's gonna be the next target, and who's gonna see those red lights?

But if you see 'em, run!

MATTERHORN'S WRINKLES

My parents and I were taking a thrilling train ride up a very famous mountain. Higher and higher, the big red train chugged up the mountainside. Mommy said, "This evening, we're gonna see the real Matterhorn," and "It's much bigger than that Disneyland ride you were on." I remembered riding it. But now, we were heading up the real mountain. Ooooh-weeee.

Almost everyone on the train had skis, but others had cameras.

They had lots of neat shops below, but all I saw from the train were pretty white hills. Daddy told me, "They're mountains," and he whispered, "We're in the Monta Rosa area of the Pennine [Swiss] Alps, little man." I thought, *Wherever we are, it's freezing; my hands are icy cold, and my teeth are chattering.*

Mommy told Daddy, "The Matterhorn should be breathtaking at sunset!"

So, I asked them, "Is that why it's getting darker?"

She answered, "We're also going up behind the mountain, and it's so big it's partly blocking out the sun, honey."

I was having lots of fun, except something was wrong; every time I gazed over, the ol' conductor was glaring right through me. He was older than Nana, and his face was ultra wrinkled, like an old raisin. *Too much sun?* I wondered. *Guess I'll call him Mr. Sunshine.* Weirdly, I couldn't stop glancing his way either. And now, he was attempting to stab his beady, little eyes right through me. *Why's he staring at me? Doesn't he like cute little six-year-old boys sitting very quietly with their parents?*

I couldn't stop looking at him, and right then, the old man barked out something weird and almost gagged.

"He's speaking German," Daddy said.

So, I asked him, "Doesn't he speak English, Daddy? What's *German*?"

The man probably heard me because he shot me another mean look. I was scared! But giggling, I looked his way again. Ha-ha, Mr. Sunshine!

Three long, squiggly hairs hang over his bony, pointed head. Then, he glared at me, pointed to a sign hanging above him, and continued to visually drill holes into my head. I learned the ABCs early, so Daddy proudly told everybody, "My boy's smart."

The sign said, "The train will not stop once it starts moving!" I was the only one who seemed to notice.

Curious, I asked Daddy, "Why doesn't the choo choo stop once it starts?"

He answered, "The Swiss are diligent about being exactly on time; it's a source of great pride for them."

Then, the conductor shouted, "Dis da last train!"

But Mommy and Daddy didn't hear him because they were too busy looking outside at "all the beautiful panoramas."

Turning around, Mr. Sunshine was, once more, beaming at me. I wanted to shout, "Daddy, stop the old man from scaring me!"

But the conductor pointed and said, "*Achtung* [notice]. The Matterhorn!"

I laughed. *Acccchhhhtunnne!* It sounded like an order. But maybe, it was.

The next thing I knew, the train stopped, everyone got off, and I heard Mommy scream!

"What's the matter, Mommy?" I yelled.

She said, "Look over there, baby; it's the real Matter-horn!"

I spun around, but I couldn't see anything. When I could see something, there was a big upside-down pizza-slice type, with a white and light blue hard rock inside. It stretched way above a million snowy mountains. I shouted, "Whaa-whoo! The mountains are all around me!"

When I got closer, the Matterhorn seemed molded into a cupped hand turned inward. But the snow was rock solid, and it really was blue! Mommy told me, "It's so cold and windy up here it turns everything a deep, shiny, aqua blue."

Rubbing my gloves together, I chattered, "Mommy, I already know it's really cold up here."

Daddy told me, "The wind shaped the Matterhorn by blowing all around it for a zillion years." He taught me, "We're up so high, at almost 14,700 feet, nothing stops the freezing, cold winds from blowing so hard."

That was when I looked down.

"Yikes!" I yelled. The bottom must be way down there. It was so far down I couldn't see the bottom!

It must have been a little while later when Mommy

asked me, "Take a picture of us, baby? It's almost sunset!" That was when I looked into her camera, but suddenly, everything got dopily weird really, really fast!

When I looked through the lens, I wasn't looking at Mommy or Daddy anymore; my attention was immediately drawn to my left, and I could barely believe what I was seeing. Everybody was gone, and "da last train" was leaving! What? This couldn't be real.

My parents were occupied; Mommy was showing Daddy more of the scenic mountains, and I was strangely captivated by "da last train" still moving. That was when I saw the mean, ol' conductor shouting at me! But I couldn't hear what he was saying. That was when it hit me: da last train was leaving without us!

I wasn't even thinking when I bolted for the train. But it was so far away, and when I got closer, Mr. Sunshine screamed, "*Verboten!*" and pushed his hands out at me. I didn't know what that meant, so I just kept running for the train and yelling, "Stop, please!"

By the time I finally got near the train, I was breathless and sucking air. As he stood at the lead car, the conductor repeated, "*Verboten.*"

So, again, I screamed back, "Stop, Mister! You just can't leave us here!" But when I tried to reboard the train, the conductor crashed into me again. He pushed me off the train, screeching, "*Achtung*! I no stop dis train, little boy!"

I couldn't stop now, so I willed myself to move. Still very confused, I ran for the train again. But this time, I went at the man headfirst. When I got to the door, the conductor pushed me away again. But this time, he pushed me so hard that I fell on the hard, packed snow and hurt my arm. I still couldn't believe he was letting da last train leave without us!

I realized, *I have only one chance to do something smart. If not, we'll all freeze to death up here.* So, defiantly, I headed for da last train one last time. This time, Mr. Sunshine and I were enemies, and my plan was much better!

When I got close this time, I yelled, "*Verboten!*" and for a split second, he was startled. Then, he shouted back, "*Nein, Kinder.*" When he went to push me, I made a zigzag move, and I leaned my bony, little shoulder right at his paunchy stomach. Because he was so much stronger than me, I thought it wouldn't work. But it did.

He pushed me down on the floor of the train, but I, this little six-year-old, proved how smart Daddy said I was; when I fell, I cried out, "Mommy!" And I knew ol' Mr. Sunshine heard me because he quickly stopped da last train! I suppose it does stop for emergencies?

Then, the wrinkled, old conductor rushed over to me, with my parents following right on his heels. My mom was distraught and said, "What's the matter, honey?"

Obviously, I told her, "When I fell on the train, I must have hurt my arm."

To my astonishment, I laughed inside, and ol' Mr. Sunshine suddenly winked at me (just between us). He was using code to let me know, "Okay, smart little boy. You got me!"

I was amazed, and I winked back at my former foe! Without knowing much, Mommy and Daddy carried me on board and got me settled. And, by the time we got back down, I was much better.

Before we left the station, we all smiled at the Matterhorn lit up by a gorgeous sunset. As Mommy mused, it was really "breathtaking" (whatever that means). Then Daddy asked me, "Wasn't this da last train, kiddo?" Then, he figured it out and whispered to Mommy, "If our darling little man didn't get hurt, we could have been stranded up here all night."

I thought, *Huh, Daddy? That's right. I am so smart. And I don't quit either.*

On the way down the mountain, I looked over at my new friend, the ol' conductor. He looked at me, too, and a sinister smile spread evenly over his weather-beaten face. I must have been an honorable opponent, so we winked at each other again. Slowly (so he'd understand me), I joked, "Achtung! Let's go, Mr. Conductor! Dis train no stop after it's moving."

He laughed uncontrollably and told me, "No. Dis train no stop for anyone else but you smart little man. Hee-hee. You really got me."

TREVOR'S SQUEEZE (A PROGRESSIONAL TALE)

My turn at bat, and I step into the batter's box in my super rad uniform. Luckily, our coach yells that the opposing pitcher can't throw strikes. As I hunch over the plate, my long legs probably fool him because he really can't find his strike zone with me obstructing him.

"Ball four," yells the umpire. Yay!

Whoo-hoo! I strut down to first base without even swinging at one pitch. And holding that huge bat isn't fun at all. All I wanted was to look great, like A-Rod clobbering another homer while everyone cheered me on.

Someday I'll hit better. But Coach says, "You gotta see your pitch, Trevor, low and right down the middle first." Until then, I'll keep schmoozing pitchers into walking me again and again.

"Walking is better anyway," Dad says. "You have a great eye, Trevor."

My dad knows I hate practicing! He's always telling me, "Do it this way." But I'm not ready yet! Even after all those hundreds of practice balls he threw me, I still walk. Hmmm. Thank God. He gave me a great eye for facing lousy pitching!

The opposing pitcher must have thought I was stealing second as I took a long lead off first base and kept a watchful eye on him, too. He probably thinks I'm clumsy with these gangly-looking legs. But he doesn't know I'm really a "sup-o-fast" rocketman. Talk about "Godspeed."

Coach shouts, "Move it over fast to second if it's a grounder, Trevor!" But I knew that already. Thankfully, I predict, *If I steal second base and slide headfirst into it, my jazzy red, white, and blue batting gloves will save me.*

I see Dad's here now. He tells people, "My headstrong boy plays his own game." My mom also proudly says, "He marches to his own drum" (whatever that means). I really love baseball, and most of the time, I think I play awesome.

I figure our cleanup batter, Rusty Boxman, will knock me over to second base anyway. And if I score, we'll win (and I'll be the undisputed hero of the planet). Cool beans! Rusty, then, bounced it to the second baseman, who, lucky for our team, booted it all the way into right field.

Lucky me, Speed Racer's flying now. And my wheels quickly get me around second base so I can zip into third base standing up! That'll show everyone I'm not "gawky." Now, even though I thought I was blazing around these bases, I wondered, *Why's their third baseman getting ready to tag me out? Why does he already have the baseball in his glove?* Oops!

I'll just slide right underneath him as Coach taught us.

Yippee, I'm—"Safe!" yells the stocky-looking umpire. *Whew-wee. That was close,* I thought. But my uniform has a great, big gash in it now, and my left knee's bleeding. Oh-weee. How did that happen? I must have slid into third base wrong, and my coach always says, "Practice makes perfect." Huh? Perfect what? Praying? Serving?

I'm almost home now, and with ungodly pride, I think, *Trevor's looking hot.* Still, it's my time to show my coach what I'm made of, as Daddy says. Plus, Coach really wanted Bobby Berkshire (his favorite) to hit instead of me. Thank God for the "everybody must play" rule. It's extra fantastic for kids like me!

Right then, Coach flashes me my sign. By running his arm down his left leg, he's telling me to race home and "do the squeeze"! *Huh? Me? You gotta be kidding me, Coach?*

I yell, "Time out," and wander over to him into the third base's coaching box. Shyly, I ask him, "Right now, you really want me to perform the squeeze, Coach?"

He's mostly silent, but he still whispers to me, "Read the signs, Trevor; then, you'll know what to do. Okay? Now, get back to third base."

Back at third base, he flashes me the same sign. I am helplessly wondering, *What's he thinking? I'm a scrawny little kid. But I'm not really all that lightning fast. Oh, well. I guess I'll just race home as fast as is humanly possible and see what happens.*

The *squeeze*: the trick is to blaze home before the pitcher can throw the ball to his catcher and he tags me out. Anyway, Coach gave me that sign, so I can't ignore it! For a second, it made me remember Mrs. Church telling us about Moses; he came down from that mountain, holding the Ten Commandments. Of those two big chiseled-stone signs, she warned us all, "Follow them precisely!"

I figured, *No doubt. This pitcher's mine!*

Realistically, when he's doing his "windup," I'm off to his right and, practically, invisible to him. My philosophy is to start zooming home before he pitches it. And my only job is to tag home plate right before their catcher tags me!

The pitcher winds up, and that's when I start explosively racing home. But I stumble, and the pitcher sees me!

Ugh. Then, he throws the ball to his catcher, who's running right at me.

Sarcastically, I blurt out, "Even better!"

In baseball terms, this situation is called a "rundown," and the catcher is almost tagging me out. Double oops! All anyone on the third baseline needs to do is "tag" me with the baseball, and I'm out. No "hero" title for me today.

I panic but squeeze out, *Be smart! And do something very quickly, or you're one, tagged-out, little man.* Then, I realize a strategy, and I shout to the catcher, "Come and get me!" Likewise, when I bolted back to third base, he threw the ball to the third baseman. But the third baseman bobbled it (toward the left-field fence) and, luckily, away from home plate!

Quickly! That's my one chance to blaze home superfast. But that's also when everything starts to suddenly slow down. I see dirt flying; my heart is pounding in my chest; my feet are going as fast as I can make them go, and everyone is yelling at me, "Go, Trevor! Run faster!" Also, you should have seen the catcher's eyes bulge. Then, the umpire slid into position, and I saw my legs fly out.

My lead cleat made a loud whooshing sound when it deftly brushed over home plate a mere millionth of a second before the catcher's glove hit my chest. Finally, back in the moment, the ump yelled, "Safe!" Wow-wee!

My screaming fans ran over to me and scooped me up on their shoulders and yelled out, "Trevor's our hero."

My dad caught me beaming and told me later, "Practice does make perfect, little man. Way to hustle out there, Speedy Gonzales? He almost caught you at third base, though." I guess that wasn't Coach who taught me that wise saying.

That was when Coach yelled, "Next stop: Pizzaland!"

"Good for me," said I as I patted my stomach.

I was certainly blessed today, and it's such a great feeling to do well for others in the sight of God. We learned in church that when you do what you're supposed to do, you'll be richly rewarded with blessings from above. However, I didn't know that included baseball and pizza.

LITTLE EMERALD

Owen was born on an early misty morning in May. His eyes were the most beautiful cobalt blue I've ever seen, and our lives haven't ever been the same. With every physical change, he's more beautiful to me. I still proudly say, "I deeply love my son," and I love all our moments together. Without being too sappy: I've always been extremely happy being his daddy!

Owen was long-awaited. It wasn't our season when we tried to start a family. And it got to the point we accepted we might never be parents. But in the late summer of 1997, a miracle happened; we were finally expecting. Whenever I remember telling our whole family, a Cheshire grin finds its way all over my face. I remember they were a lot happier than us, knowing Owen was very unexpected. He, truly, was our long-answered prayer and a miracle sent from God!

Before Owen's birth, we thought we were having a baby girl. We even picked two very nice girls' names. But just in case, we picked a boy's name, too. When Owen prematurely popped out, his mom was completely exhausted. But in shock, I looked at him and stuttered, "That's no girl!" So, before another anxious breath, I told the attending nurse, "That's Owen James." And she immediately wrote his name on his warmer. There was no going back, so it's great we had his name waitin' in the wings.

One thing most people quickly notice about Owen is he's always smiling and laughing. He has always been that way; we have countless pictures of Owen giggling (especially with his "grammie")! I'm glad we instilled in him a sense of fun and laughter is in his genes. It's all something we have gotten back, twentyfold, from our cute boy. He's our little sparkling gem.

Owen knows how much we adore him. But because we feel so incredibly blessed to have him, our love has always been much stronger. Showering him with love made him blossom into a very goofy, loving, happy, extraordinarily special boy. But something struck me as very eerie yesterday.

Owen was almost a teenager, and I was looking for a very special gift for his birthday. I thought some sort of small boyish jewelry was appropriate (maybe with his birthstone). But I didn't know the birthstone for May. His mom's birthstone is pearl, and I had given her pearls and rubies before. But for Christmas, I gave his mom a very pretty ring with an emerald inside.

For our tenth anniversary, I gave her a very nice emerald necklace, never knowing its beguiled significance. Then, on another eventful night, I gave Owen's mom a Precious Moments figurine; it showed a little boy licking an ice-cream cone while his girl puppy was waiting for her licks.

So, recently, I asked a coworker (and a jewelry maker), "What's May's birthstone?"

I was floored when she told me, "It's an emerald!"

What's spookier is we have a boy with an emerald birthstone, and his girl puppy is always waiting by his side for her next delectable dripping-with-oodles-of-a-delicious-ice-cream treat!

Owen's having an emerald birthstone is still bizarre and eerie to me. But the irrefutable fact is he's our miracle boy and our most precious, God-given jewel. He's the most amazing little boy who we had always hoped for and passionately wanted. And nothing compares to our happy, miraculous, smiling, loving, goofy, handsome, and sweetest Little Emerald!

FUR-TEE-WI-ZER CLASS

Even though the icky, sticky humidity was drenching my shirt with gobs of sweat, we were lucky to have a decent breeze swirling around us. And with a full day's sun left, clear skies made me believe our workday was gonna go off without a hitch!

Despite the conditions, every family member had their own projects, including our sheltie, Jenni. Her guard-dog duties included barking at every neighborhood dog that innocently walked by our corner. My little boy, Owen, was also on task; his Momma asked him to keep busy and take in all the sights and sounds around the house.

As instructed, he tried to finish his lunch and cause as little trouble as possible. But his "mushee bugher" was cold even though his mom made it just the way he liked it: "Only kaz-zup; pleeeeze, Momma." The hamburger, having quickly gotten cold, stuck out of his pants' pocket like an old toy. But I was amazed anything got into his tummy other than a "piece of weely good candy, Daddy."

With Owen kinda busy (and sorta fed), his mom got busy with her "labor of love," gardening; she busied herself with weeding baby perennials enhancing our blandly painted shed. And her tulips came next. But she prayed, "God, keep Owen busy long enough for me to finish everything I want to do today."

Having enough time for anything reminded me of a coworker's sage advice: "You think this job's rough? Your real job starts when you get home!"

Sometimes I'd sit in our driveway for five minutes. Owen would stare at me, asking, "What's he doing, Momma?" followed by, "Why's Daddy just sitting in his car?"

When I finally came in, I'd sarcastically admit, "I'm getting ready for you, little boy! And you can distract me anytime you want. Deal?"

I was also quite involved with my project: trudging along, I was digging twenty eight-inch-deep holes around the base of our new sprawling purple-ash tree. Soon after moving in, we spruced up our new home with a beautiful transplanted tree. Its sole purpose was to share cooling duties with our taller sugar-maple tree. But the ash had very pretty purple-colored leaves. And lucky for us, they were both growing into magnificent shade trees.

Right after I dug my eleventh hole, with more sweat dripping down my back, it was break time; we got to thoroughly enjoy Mom's ice-cold lemonade. Owen was through with his "bugher" and happily guzzled down his mom's sweet-tasting tea (everything was "tea" to him). A smug grin crawled over his quenched face, and he weirdly surprised me by asking, "Whatcha doin', Daaaaddy?" Only seconds ago, I was thinking, *He never pays attention to me unless he's nearly falling into one of my oversized holes.*

My three-year-old continued his naturally curious inquisition with, "Why d'ya dig all those holes around my tree, Daddy?" His possessive attitude came from when we told him, "Start calling the ash 'your tree,' Owen."

We bestowed it on him by stating, "It's your tree, so it was placed right outside your room." In business, they call that "taking ownership." But we always wanted Owen to treat the tree as "my ash." Besides, when it was fully lush, his ash would be the giant tree pleasantly cooling his room. That's when he'll really appreciate it!

I loved answering all his "why this" and "why that" questions and being there for teaching moments. I explained, "I dug the holes so I could feed the tree. I need to drop some fertilizer into every hole." Then, pointing at the fertilizer, I taught Owen, "These granules contain all the nutrients your pretty purple ash needs to grow up big 'n' strong. The fertilizer is your ash's food supply, like what your mama feeds you! I guess that makes your mommy a boy-tilizer!"

I thoroughly enjoyed watching his reactions. And I heartily laughed because the words "granules" and "nutrients" gave him fits; he tried sounding each word out, and I heard him say, "What's noo-tee-antz, Daddy?"

Continuing my unplanned lesson, I told him, "They are for your first question: I'm digging all these holes to supply your tree with fertilizer."

As cute as a button, he arched up to ponder, "My tree weall-wee eats fur-tee-wi-zer, Daddy?"

It cracked me up seeing him mentally imagining his tree eating fertilizer.

"Yeah," I said. "It eats the 'fur-tee-wi-zer'" (more chuckles). I wondered, *How am I gonna continue this?* I didn't want to befuddle Owen with big words; "photosynthesis" is a hard one. But frankly, seeing him mouth each word made me laugh even more. Keeping it up, I sort of wished I had bigger words for him and me.

I knew I was being "a mean Daddy." But I believe there's nothing more adorable than Owen. Many times, the whole child-rearing process forced me to my knees; I humbly thanked God for every unforgettable memory with him, and I take full advantage of each one! Admittedly, I'm blessed to have so many incredibly great times with my little, pint-sized comedian. I honestly believe whatever good I'll ever do, God has repaid me so many times over!

My Christian grandmother was my shining example. Her favorite line was, "But for the grace of God go I being thankful for God's grace on me and leaving out some bad things."

God's grace honored us with our most precious gift! Hokey? Yes. But very true.

My little wonder sat and continued looking at the holes as I said, "A little fertilizer goes into every hole." But I was losing him when he heard, "It has to get all the way down into that hole and to your tree's roots." When he didn't understand me, I told him, "Look way down at the bottom of that hole. Can you see those thick-stick/finger thingies?"

He shook his head and stuttered, "Thaaaaaat's a woot?"

I shot back, "Yeah. They grow out from the tree's bottom, and they move the tree food directly into your tree so it can eat it up. It's sort of like a long tunnel into your tree's tummy." But I was really surprised he didn't ask me, "How do da woots help my twee eat its food? With teeth?" Instead, he stared down the hole and looked at all "da woots."

Only then, anxious to fill all the hole's "woots," he shimmied over to every hole, determined to finish his mission.

"Houston to Owen? Do ya read me? Over."

When he finished his thorough inspection, he reported, "Every hole of the ash has lots of woots, Daddy. Now my ash is ready for fur-tee-wi-zer."

This supersmart boy stupefied me because he was learning so much. Was it possible for him to now master potty training, T-ball, skydiving, or Mozart? The world is truly his oyster. It's the only thing I want for my little man; I believe a parent's job is to make each generation better-off than theirs!

Next, I muttered, "Roots carry the fertilizer's nutrients into your tree. Next lesson: water is the second thing your tree needs to grow," and before I got another word out, he said, "Big 'n' stuhwong?"

Afterward, we lavished the tree with cold water to quench its thirst!

Much of this caught me totally off guard. Then I glanced at his mom and cautiously whispered, "This is still our son, right? The bright boy who never listens to his daddy?"

Mom chuckled, shook her head, and returned to her gardening that Owen called, "Mommy's puh-witty fwow-wers." And just as if he knew what was coming next, my future Nobel Prize laureate asked me, "What's the third thing my ash needs, Daddy?"

This day, however, wasn't about lessons. But I was ecstatic to be teaching him all these insightful things. And even that scorching sun helped me with the next lesson I shared with the most beautiful student a proud daddy ever had. And Owen soaked up every word, kinda as I did with my dad.

Without missing a beat, I said, "How d'ya know there are three things?" with more laughs. His face told the tale, mirroring a puppy with its head cocked sideways when you ask him something it probably already knows. Jenni does it. But I know she knows that I know it's all an act. Jenni's also incredibly cute, so we're extremely blessed with two adorably cute kids! Nothing compares.

Pushing ahead not to lose my budding scholar's attention, I continued, saying, "The biggest nourishing ingredient for your tree"—pointing at the sun—"is that very big hot orange thing up there. Even though it heats everything else, it also uses our fertilizer and water to feed the ash. In fact, it's all your ash needs"—in unison with my little boy—"to grow up big 'n' stuhwong." Great, tree-feeding lesson done!

The way we celebrated, you'd think we just won the lottery. But his mom and I, frankly, have so much more emotional currency, with Owen paying us back every day. Plus, we cherish what he has taught us on many, many occasions!

Right then, I turned around to see something completely "quazee" (to anyone besides a three-year-old boy). With the celebration stalled, I stopped to rub my eyes because I wasn't entirely sure what I was seeing. It was so (Owen-speak) "un-be-wee-vuh-buhl."

But my eyes were not playing tricks on me; much to my surreal surprise, Owen crumpled his whole "mushee bugher" and was slowly crawling up to every hole. He said he was dropping in "gwamyules from my yucky old bugher!"

Oh, God, I thought. "What are you doing, Nutty?" said I, chuckling and shaking my head in sheer blissful amazement.

At the last hole, Owen looked down and gently whispered, "Eat these yummy hamm-bugher gwamyules, Ash. You'll love 'em. And trust me: they're way better than Daddy's fur-tee-wi-zer!"

Now I knew I'd never stop laughing again. Thank God!

Owen must have read my mind because before I could get the words "What in God's green earth are you doin', Owen?" out, he looked at me with beautiful big droopy blueish-hazelish beagle's eyes and begged me, "Can't my twee eat my leftover hammbugher just this once, Daaaad-dy?" He followed that with, "Ash needs a lot to eat, wight?"

I was happy and dumbfounded, but Owen kept blurting out so many thought-provoking questions. He thought, *Ash weally wants a dee-whi-shus beefee-hamm-bugher. He doesn't like...wha' d'ya call 'em, gwam-mee-yules, Daddy?* OMG. Someone, please, shake me?

I looked at his mom and fell to the ground, laughing myself silly. Next, he nailed me with another staggering conundrum: "Do we weally have ta put 'em in every hole, Daddy?"

Was he asking me for options? And that's where I called it "Quitsville."

I declared, "Okay, baby boy. Today's science lesson is over." I reached a point of no return, with real work still looming. Luckily, I dug all the holes, and it was time for the school bell to ring! Whew.

Then, Owen, Mommy, and even Jenni helped me throw tiny granules into each hole. We finished our job by filling 'em all with healthy topsoil. The work reunion really helped us have a "mah-vel-us" time, and Daddy said, "You have to make your own memories because they won't just happen." I thought, *This memory is gonna be one for the books!*

Owen wisely summarized, "My ash is full now."

And thankfully, we'll "be cool" for many springs and summers! I was happy imagining more fun-filled days coming our way. Then, Owen volunteered for the day's last job. (Who knew that would happen?) Scurrying over, carrying the long green garden hose, he aimed it at me.

The hose was a watering instrument, but Owen thought it was his very own fantastic toy, with never-ending water trickling down into his tiny wet shoes. I thought, *No one writes comedy like this*, and I couldn't stop laughing. Curious, I asked him, "Wazzup, budd?"

He looked at me with a weird face and announced, "My twee needs more water, Daaaaddy. Di' ya forget dat?"

Wow. Did he actually just listen to me? That was when I fell over. He knew we had to water his ash more, so I told him, "Go ahead! But make sure you water each hole weally good!" He marched off while we did other things. Surprisingly, I felt something *really* cold all the way down my freezing back!

"Aah, gee-whiz," I said, running away from Water Boy and his forty-foot water cannon.

Work was done, and this was the perfect time for good old-fashioned fun!

"Let's do this!" I yelled, chasing down my adorable son while desperately trying to get control of my troublesome tot as he squirted me until I was thoroughly drenched.

When I did catch him, I changed gears and asked him, "Wouldn't Mommy be more fun to soak? She needs a lot more cooling-off than we do!"

His conniving grin glared back at me, reminding me of my mom saying, "I've seen that smile on another devilish boy a few thousand times." Guess I'll get repaid more, too?

What utter bliss, I thought. *Sun, water, granules, "mushee hammbughers," and hilarious fun! What's better for two starving trees?*

Note to self:

1. Never buy tree fertilizer again.

2. Only use mushy, "kaz-zup-only" hamburgers

3. Forget first and second. Then, continue having oodles of fun.

NEVER ALONE

I moved into my new apartment in 2002. Then, I hesitated to go to a seminar for recovering divorcés. But the experience helped me a lot; their best advice was, "Make your home comfortable." That challenged me to relax and make my home more bearable.

I was never great at being alone, so I followed my eight-year-old son's advice and got a pet. He asked me, "Can we have a pet at your house?" But I can't have dogs, so I started looking for a loveable little kitty. And luckily, it wasn't too long before someone gave me one by chance.

A coworker found a one-year-old black-and-white kitty he could not keep. My gain was a friendly male, and he was just what the doctor (my son) ordered. Owen named his cat "Rufus," but "Skunk" or "Oreo" seemed better. Alas, "Rufus" won out. I found an Irish saint named Rufus (and our whole family is mostly Irish), so the name stuck.

Many afternoons Owen sat with Rufus purring in his lap. It was cute seeing them watching their favorite cartoons together. Even *Kim Possible* had her sidekick.

Owning a pet is work but cleaning his litter box wasn't bad compared to the joy Rufus gave us. I had always been content being alone, but I noticed my bed still felt empty. And my whole apartment seemed too quiet. But it finally dawned on me when Rufus showed up that continuous silence disappeared.

He also surprised me the first night he jumped up on my bed; Rufus lay right in the crook of my arm. Who knows? Maybe, we felt safe together. But it seemed as if we had been doing it for a while. I also loved him feeling safe with me.

Other times he'd lay on my arm while we watched TV, or he'd curl up on his blanket and watch birds play outside. Then, sometimes, I'd hear him purring, and seconds later, he'd be mixin' in my lap and looking for a sweet spot to take a cat nap. I loved naps; now, I had a real cat to enjoy them.

I always hear people who adopt pets say they were "rescued." I guess we both needed rescuing! Rufus hated the winter cold, and unconsciously, we were both fortunate to be each other's rescue buddy. When I remember each time Rufus gave me a rare kiss, I smile because it's his saying, "Thanks, buddy. But don't get too soppy about it, okay?"

However, I could never know Rufus wasn't going to be my only pet.

I always thought, *If you have a cat, fish aren't the next logical choice.* But I couldn't get that across to my needy eight-year-old son. A while ago, someone gave me a one-gallon fishbowl. Why?

Then, my son won a big goldfish at his school's carnival and remembered, "Daddy has a fishbowl." He walked straight into my apartment with a very large goldfish swimming in a bulging bag of fishy water and asked me, "Daddy, where's your fishbowl?"—the answer to the "why?"

Owen never missed a beat; he fished through my cabinets until he found the missing goldfish bowl. And his next stumper was, "What water do goldfish use, Daddy?"

When did I become a fish expert?

His mom said, "They use cold water."

So, we filled his bowl, and Owen informed me, "We gotta go to the pet store for fish stuff" (bluish rocks, goldfish food, and a sunken ship for Goldie). Ugh! The goldfish already had a name? Can that be good?

Surely, I didn't know if Rufus even wanted Goldie, so I put his fishbowl up out of his reach. I knew Rufus was well-fed and lazy, so I thought, *He wouldn't wanna exert himself for that climb*. That night, I had to admit, it was more relaxing watching Goldie float around in his bejeweled bowl, with Rufus purring in my lap. And even though fishbowl cleaning isn't fun, Goldie was worth it.

Sparingly, I thought one fish was fine. But that didn't jive with my son's curious nature. And without telling me, Owen already decided, *We're going to Walmart for more fish*. Only, he asked me, "Can we buy some more Hot Wheels, Daddy?"

The next day we were in the toy aisle right next to the pet center. That was where Owen laid his trap; he said, "I'm gonna look at some fish, okay?" and I hustled there to check out this latest situation. Superquick, and without me knowing anything, he had already chosen a few tropical fish as a clerk poured them into more bags. Huh?

Then, the clerk asked me, "Cash or credit?"

I pulled out my wallet and, sarcastically, asked Owen, "Shouldn't we get these more expensive fish, dude?" He chuckled, but I didn't.

When I first saw Owen's fish, they were lovely. "But more pets?" I asked him.

Seeing the gleam in his pretty blue eyes answered

my question. He proudly said, "They can all go in with Goldie!"

But the helpful clerk specifically advised me, "Those tropical fish require a heated tank." Then, he pointed down the aisle and said, "You need a ten-gal heated tank like that aquarium over there."

Wow! Until recently, wasn't I all alone? Surprisingly, over just a few months, I have a cat, a goldfish, and even more freshwater fish. Again, ugh!

Also, I didn't know anything about assembling a heated fish tank. But now, I needed to install everything in a workable fashion, except I'm not good at setting anything up; I can't even change my oil. However, none of that matters to an enterprising eight-year-old who builds complex Lego fortresses without directions. Why wasn't he setting it up? Fortunately, I got our new tank "swim-ready."

"Well, lookee here! We have a real, live, working fish tank."

But Owen wasn't impressed, and he fired back, "Why'd it take you soooo long?" He also slammed me with, "Burnt, Daddy."

Miraculously to myself, I just achieved a minor feat in DIY/pet ownership. But all Owen wanted was to splash his new fish in his new tank.

"Why do I need all these pets?" I asked him.

From somewhere far away, he scorched, "You can teach an old dog new tricks?"

Huh? Now you're adding dogs to our ever-growing family?

Nonetheless, if you saw my sweet son's face watching his freshwater fish swim around, it was incredibly blissful and utterly sweet. Plus, the fish were beautiful and very calming. But his longer fish tank needed my grandma's antique heirloom, the sewing machine, to sit on.

On another trip to Walmart, I was hoodwinked again (more fish food, supplies, nets, special rocks, and more underwater accessories). Great. Also, cleaning the fish tank was extremely filthy, not fun, and time-consuming! But compared to watching the pretty fish scurry around, it wasn't all that bad. Owen, however, always wants to touch his fish.

Unfortunately, at that same time, we prematurely lost Owen's sheltie and his beloved sister, Jenni. None of us could have imagined her loss or how much it would hurt! It was excruciatingly heartbreaking, but it was much worse for Owen; missing Jenni was agonizing, and even though he didn't pay much attention to her when he was younger, he and Jenni became close buddies.

One night, Owen told me, "Jenni wakes me up every morning with her cold nose and a kiss," and "I really miss her." Even now, Owen occasionally chokes up and tells me, "I miss Jenni."

I think he wonders if I have forgotten Jenni. So, I whisper, "I do, too, baby. Every day!"

That was why I went to a rescue shelter recently, hoping to find a nice dog who'd ease our troubled hearts. I looked for smaller dogs but didn't find one. However, on the far wall, I glimpsed a very small, petrified, red-colored, foxlike, pure-bred Pomeranian puppy. He was visibly and fiercely shaking and begging me, "Please, Mister, get me outta here?" But they had him on a medical hold, so I couldn't take him home.

They did let me walk him around, though, and you should have seen how deliriously happy he was to be free. Talk about extremely loveable, too. When I came back to return him, he began shaking again. It was as if he was asking me, "Dude. Why aren't we breakin' outta here?" Luckily, a month later, he was ours (and Owen was unaware).

The next time Owen visited me, this little eight-pound pup shimmied up to him, stood up on his back legs, and sweetly kissed Owen. My son was understandably shaken, and he stuttered, "Aw, it's a cute puppy."

Without being able to contain myself, I admitted, "Hold him, kiddo? He's yours."

Owen's jaw dropped, and he mouthed, "Is he really mine?"

I have never sat in awe of a happier moment with my boy other than his birth! Each time I sat still and cried happy tears.

The boy and the puppy bonded immediately. And seconds later, they were outside, playing. My son named him "Ralphie" (after Ralph Kramden) because he said, "He's red. So, I wanted him to keep an *R* in his name." But Owen wondered aloud, "Is Ralphie replacing Jenni?"

With tears running down my cheeks, I answered, "I could never replace Jenni-poo. Ralphie's his own dog; we'll love him the same way we loved Jenni." That seemed to lessen Owen's anxiety.

It's hard to explain Ralphie other than he's 1,000 percent goofy. He's all puppy; he spins and hops up on our bed and dances around, at actually ten years old. Honestly, he has made me laugh 10,000 times. He never sits still and loves massages in between wiping his nose with his legs the cute way dogs always do.

At night we cuddle, and Ralphie lies on his back and pushes out his front paws as if he's playing this weird game only he knows. But he wants other people to play along! He loves women ("A regular chick magnet," Owen says); he licks us repeatedly, and our two newest rescued buddies have occasional sparring sessions. But most of the time, they get along. I've even seen Rufus try to kiss Ralphie.

They're weird, too, because each pet seems as if the other pet isn't there. They're (lone) "top dog" and (sole) "top cat." I suppose they make it work. Rufus tolerates Ralphie as Garfield shines on his cartoon dog. Plus, Ralphie's hilarious to watch; he kinda acts like Garfield's dog, galloping and prancing around "dum-dee-dee-dum." He's playacting, "I don't have one problem, only happy times." Post-shelter, nothing seems to bother him, and Ralphie's mostly the picture of happiness.

He makes me silly, too, and that has dramatically changed my life. I give him loads of love, and it's great to realize I still have gobs of love to give. I love him, and it's incredibly magnificent to share his "puppy love." The best reward is getting all the love back fiftyfold! It's nothing taking him for walks, and having Owen's pets here makes me feel extremely happy and never alone.

But the other day, Owen was over, and I didn't sleep well the night before. Likewise, I was uncharacteristically cranky. Usually, whenever I ask Owen to take care of his pets, he answers quickly with an unmistakable "no." He's not being sarcastic; he really believes it's not his responsibility, and he really does not want to do it. Simple. And even though it's no big deal, it bothers me in a weird way.

Later the next morning, I asked him, "Could you feed your fish?" Another "no" followed, and it elicited a stark response: "Isn't this the 200,000th time I'm feeding your fish?" I followed that up with: "You have some nerve, little boy." Owen kept quiet. A smart coping response?

I was making lunch later, and Owen and Ralphie were horseplaying on the couch. I asked him, "Could you, please, take Ralphie out? He really needs to go."

But a quick "no" flew back at me. When I finished our sandwiches, I took Ralphie out. And then, I asked Owen, "Every now and then, I could use your help with your pets." But he laughed! Supposedly, I must have bored him in the past with my countless unresponsive and unpersuasive requests.

And that was why I saved Owen's best job for last, hoping I'd get the last laugh. With a plastic bag in hand, I marched over to Owen and informed him, "It's your turn to clean out Rufus's litter box, buddy!"

Lightning fast, another "no" flew at me. Then, he rattled off, "You gotta be kidding me, Dad. Rufus's box is nasty and stinky."

That was when all my sleeplessness caught up with me and extended me way past the universal boiling point. I was way past frustrated and was getting madder. I looked at my apathetic, defiant son and hollered, "Owen, all these pets are yours! Why am I always taking care of them?"

Still, my unhelpful son looked at me dumbstruck. That face was quickly replaced with a quirky-looking grin that fell over his entire determined face. His next words floored me! He said, "Duh, Dad! You don't really get it, do you? All these pets are for you! I got them for you to take care of you whenever I'm not here. I just wanted you never to be alone, Daddy!"

I was stunned and broke down crying. It instantly reminded me of a four-year-old Owen rushing out to hug me when I was leaving our home for the last time. All along, Owen was taking special care of his daddy. Dang. It blew me away. And as the realization continued hitting me, my heart melted. He was right; my smart, loving, extremely thoughtful boy was only concerned about his daddy's heart all along. He has been doing it ever since I left—one pet at a time! Thank You, God. Nothing's better than this!

Now, I was dumbfounded, and I sat there thinking, *Huh! I'll be a monkey's uncle (no monkeys, too—we already have enough pets). Granted, I really miss my boy when he's not here. But my pets do a fantabulous job looking after me until we get to see Owen's funny face again. We all look forward to his return. Then, we're all a silly, happy crew again. And you never know what'll happen!*

That evening Owen helped me clean Rufus's litter box, and I apologized for being mad. Then I pulled him close with everything I had. "Thank you very much, honey bear," poured out of me, adding, "You did an incredible job of caring for me all this time. I love you so much, especially for not wanting me to be alone. Now, please, feed your fish."

I was shocked there wasn't a quick "no." Instead, Owen shot back, "Okay, Daddy. But just this once; after all, they're your fish!"

Sometime later that night, I was sitting in my favorite glider chair (excuse me: "everyone's favorite glider chair"); Ralphie lies on top of it almost every day, and Rufus likes to lie in it and absorb the hot sun during his after-noon naps. Obviously, Owen loves it, too.

I was reclining in everyone's chair and enjoying a movie. Then, Ralphie and Rufus both climbed up on me. Ralphie found his comfy spot above me, and Rufus mixed until he, too, found his comfiest spot. You should have seen that hallmark moment. I couldn't be alone now, even if I tried! And I'm so glad I'm never alone. Love and concern are with me, and peace is all around me.

Thanks again, Master Owen!

OVER AND OVER

Pam wakes up on another beautiful morning. She really loves living in her early-Victorian home and strolling through her self-styled rooms. But what she really loves is having everything in its place. With hard work, her house always smells like fresh-picked lilies.

However, things would be much easier to maintain if she didn't also live with a very active seven-year-old boy she affectionately calls "Cyclone"; he earned the name because after he has run through it, the house always looks as if it has been hit by gale-force winds. Unfortunately, Billy has never disappointed her; he forever leaves destruction in his wake.

Before Pam has even had her first cup of coffee, she's already annoyed. She yells down to Billy, "Your bed's not made, so please, make it, sweetie!" Then, it only takes seconds for her to march down the stairs toward the kitchen and lean over to pick up Billy's pj's.

That's where she finds the refrigerator and the Lucky Charms cereal box wide-open and a half-filled bowl of Cap'n Crunch sitting on the granite counter.

"Hey, young man, make your bed now and clean these dishes up, okay?"

"Yeah, Mommy," echoes down the hall.

But today's chores aren't close to motivating her lanky blond-haired boy. If anything, he's working harder to liberate himself from anything not fun!

Later that morning, Pam's busy doing another load of laundry, and she notices Ralphie's water dish is empty. Also, the thirty-pound bag of dog food is lying all over the floor. The revelation suddenly propels Pam into the front hallway, where she catches an eyeful of Billy's toys (trucks and muscle cars) "all over tarnation," as Billy's granddad says.

Now more determined, she tells Billy, "Get in here and put these toys away, now." And, "Dude! Please, refill your dog's food and water dishes!"

On her way out to the mailbox, Pam hears a subtle "yeah, Mom." But without checking whether Billy's finished, she chats up her neighbor friend, Suzie, and heads toward the den to check her emails.

That's when Ralphie's leash catches her eye; she sees Billy's Spiderman drawings blanketing the TV table, and Billy's Nintendo Wii components are spread out all over the floor, with his joystick and wires. Sitting outside, the family hamper welcomes her to a muddy pair of jeans, too. That makes her momentarily think, *I can't believe my not-so-funny, messy kid!*

When lunchtime approaches, Pam gets more perturbed. After she summons her Boy Wonder, he meekly comes up to her, and she says, "Young man, I want all this cleaned up before you do anything else. Do you hear me? Is anyone listening in there?" tapping on his head.

Standoffs, like this morning's joust, have, regretfully, happened too many times before. So, Billy concedes, "I'll do it, Mommy," hoping his "Mommy" is magic to her ears.

"Ditch the cornball stuff," she says. "Just. Get. It. Done. Pronto! Got it?"

For lunch, Pam prepares Billy's favorite. She hopes her little guy has finished his chores. And while he's downing his fave grill-cheese sandwich, she checks his handiwork. Then, she again returns frustrated after blowing out a very maddening "argh." After collecting herself, she asks Billy, "What's the matter, kiddo? Why did you only do a few things I asked you to do?"

His sad blue eyes betray him when he, overdramatically, blurts out, "Okayyy, Mom. I'll do it. Gee-whizz already!"

The day's still gorgeous, so Pam decides she'll hang her sheets outside and goes about busying herself with that. Meanwhile, Billy's snack time is over, and Pam heads to her office. There she's aghast to find her formerly clean worktable is now littered with Oreo wrappers and all the wires got exposed when Billy moved her monitor again, and she cringes out, "That little menace!"

All these calamities make her pause for a second, growl, and realize, "Billy's been playing Farmville. He has made another mess. I can't take this anymore. He needs to stop!" And mounting frustration causes her to strut into the front hallway where Billy's playing.

He has, obviously, not picked up anything. But even though she's past annoyed, she calmly leans down, looks into his cute green eyes, and roars, "Billy, do I have to keep asking you, over and over, to clean up your things, then watch you get it done completely?"

"Nah, Mommy," he relinquishes. "I'm sorry, and I'll do it right away."

Her son's compliance makes her feel some progress is being made, and Billy slowly heads for the family room with Pam on his heels.

"I don't want to watch you either, Billy. But how many

times do I have to say, 'pick up your clothes,' 'put your toys away,' and 'clean up your messes'? You're a big boy now. I don't have to check up on you all the time, do I?"

Hoping she has finally gotten through to Mr. Pigpen, Pam's heart softly hums. Then, she prays, "God, make this a small victory for me and my little nut!" Despite the day's numerous frustrations, Billy's moderate surrender earns his mom a chance to halfheartedly believe, *One day, he'll do what I ask when I ask him.* That's followed by a questionable laugh, and she wonders, *Who am I kidding?* and *When's that gonna happen?* Moms can only hope, right?

An hour later, Pam walks into her sitting room, gazes at the stylish décor, and simultaneously trips over Billy's shin guards, soccer cleats, and multicolored soccer ball. Also, she sees his big Ryder truck surrounded by a makeshift battlefield. And on her *new* foyer floor, she sees literally a million tiny green soldiers scrambling around. Pam shrieks, "Okay, grunt! It's war, now. But I have the biggest gun!"

She frantically picks up a flowery pillow, buries her head in it, and muffles a discouraged primal scream (and slowly counts to 1,000). Along the way, she wonders, *How do I persuade my Prince of Mayhem to pick things up without telling him repeatedly? Surely, I'm not the only mom experiencing this continually exasperating situation?*

And although it's way too late, Pam has reached a boiling point.

"It's time to square off with Master Messy."

Pam turns Billy around and begins with, "I'm at my wits' end with you, little boy. This charade must stop now! Do you hear me, Billy?"

When Billy finally senses his mom's meter has skyrocketed, he begins picking up his mess. But it's way too late; Pam lifts him up and strongly says, "William Taylor Jennings! You have not done a thing I've asked you to do today! Do you, honestly, need me telling you what to do 20,000 times a day? It's time you started picking up your own mess! Once that's done, you can play. It's eeezey once you get the hang of it. Okey-dokey?"

His mom's beaming smile tells Billy she isn't mad anymore. So, he cleans up everything while she fixes the family a nice dinner. When he's done, he tells her, "It's all done," and, "All I wanted to do was goof off today. So, I'm sorry it took me forever to get it all done."

Within minutes, Pam's husband comes home, and they both rush over to see him. He's equally happy to see them. But he blurts out, "Wow, it's nice in here." Following that, he notices, "It smells so fresh in here, too. Have you guys been working hard all day?"

That's when Billy pipes up, "Yeah, Dad. I helped Mommy clean up everything," winking at his mom.

After eating a scrumptious-tasting dinner, watching a little television, and taking a sunset walk, they all go to bed in their clean, comfy, and fresh-smelling home.

The next morning Pam wakes up in her sun-drenched bedroom and prays for a much better day today. Sashaying around her upstairs, she thinks, *The house, surprisingly, hasn't changed a bit*. Then, she stutters, "Whew-wee. All righty then." But once she ventures into Billy's bathroom, things take a much darker turn.

Right away, Pam notices Billy's toothbrush sitting on the toilet with gobs of toothpaste spread all over the vanity. Next, she stares at something undeniably hideous: piled high in the middle of Billy's bedroom floor are Rollerblades, a skateboard, arm pads, and Billy's scooter ("Things that should be, safely, put away"). Yesterday's shirt is also lying on Billy's unmade bed.

Utterly discouraged, Pam stops, collects herself while a scream rises in her throat, and spews to herself, "What am I going to do with you, bugger?" With her newest discovery, Pam places her hands on her hips, shakes her head, rolls her eyes, and vows, "Here we go again, little man! But watch out, buster, cause it's on, now! Billyyy!"

BATTING PRACTICE

It was a very sticky summer evening. The tall fifty-foot green maple trees hovered over Trevor like long sticks of broccoli with thick emerald-green handlike heads.

Trevor, all eight years old of him, sleek and gangly, slowly walked up to home plate. Watching him maneuver his awkward four-foot frame made someone surmise even a grazing turtle could move faster. Everything on Trevor was long, though, including his skinny arms and legs. Even his basketball shorts hung way down to even bonier calves.

Sporting short-cropped dark-brown hair, some said, "He's handsome enough to be on TV," as his dad was waiting to pitch to him.

In a squeaky voice, Trevor said, "Wait a minute. I gotta get set." He was busy shuffling his feet. Then, he lowered his bony knees that were slightly covered by his long sparkling-white Phillies T-shirt.

His bat was heaved over his sloping shoulders, and he arched his back only to grunt, "Wow, Dad. This is heaveee." Swinging his bat right at his dad was also quite an effort. And every time Mighty Trevor swung, he brought his bat back and locked it into a Pete Rose position. Pete Rose, known to everyone as "Charlie Hustle," was Trevor's favorite baseball player and present hero!

Style wasn't lost on Trevor either; his coach even said, "If you look good, you play even good-er." So, on both hands, Trevor sported gleaming white-and-blue batting gloves; they helped him steady his bat. And frequently, he'd bring the bat up high while his tiny hands tightly gripped the bat's knob.

One of his skinny elbows pointed right at his dad, and the other one was aimed right back at the silver chain-link backstop. This night, however, was just Trevor and his dad having batting practice. His dad asked him, "Ready?" and Trevor excitedly shouted, "Yep, Daddy-O."

Then, he leaned his scrawny body over home plate, pointed his bat right at a spot over it, and asked his dad, "Put it right there, Dad," meaning waste high. Imitating Bobby Bonds, Trevor bravely stated, "If you put it right there, it's a goner!" As instructed, his dad delivered the pitch to Trevor's requested spot, and Trevor's eyes bulged open really wide!

He hunched up on the tiptoes of his new stylishly red

Converse sneakers. And as he swung his bat at the speeding ball, the two came together, and the cataclysmic collision made a resoundingly loud whack! After hearing that, Trevor's dad blew his bubble and said, "Another grounder, son. Swing level, Trevor, as we practiced!"

The little boy only half listened to his dad coaching, "And choke up more! We don't have a lot of baseballs." After Trevor smacked some more grounders, they both retrieved them, although Trevor didn't need to go far —most of his baseballs landed behind him!

Trevor also discovered some foul balls rolled another twenty-five feet behind the playground's metal honeycombed backstop. Slowly but surely, Trevor strolled over to them. It was a classic, Norman Rockwell-like snapshot of a slow-moving, lazy little boy who can't wait to do his homework.

When batting practice was over, Trevor had a leisurely catch with his dad. You could tell Trevor was just learning that art, too. His hands were very small; it seemed like his whole body could fit inside his oversized glove. So, it was unusually hard for him to catch the ball.

When the dad threw the ball to his son, it looked as if Trevor was willing the ball to fly into his glove; he held his glove up and out over his head. Then, he jogged around and vertically pushed his glove up. Using Trevor's method, the only way he'd catch the ball was if the ball was metal and his glove was some giant magnet. He didn't give up trying, though!

Shortly after missing the ball again, Trevor announced, "I'm tired, Dad. Can we go home now?" That was when his dad pulled out some Gatorade and Life Savers and told Trevor, "Okay. That's enough practice for tonight. We'll do it again sometime soon, okay?"

Trevor coughed out a husky, "Great, Dad. I can't wait! But I'm beat now! The Gatorade was refreshing, but it tasted kinda tart, Dad! Anyway, what are the Life Savers for?"

CHOICES

The most decisive choice a Christian must make is whether or not to use their free will and His gifts to help others. We each make many choices in our lives, and each one comes with its own eternal and earthy consequences.

For instance, I always wondered, "What's it like to be a deer in the headlights? And what's it really like to see a car coming right for you, knowing there's nothing you can do?" Are (bulging-eyed) deer inherently aware, "Just stand there and let it happen," or do they quickly rationalize, "Anyway, I don't have any control over this"?

If I saw a car speeding straight at me, I hope my first reaction would be to run! I pondered, "Does shock make the deer stand still, or are they more practical than us?" Running seems futile, and they probably think, *It's an unfeasible attempt to change an inevitably perilous conclusion!* Either way, too many deer freeze. Regardless of that, I still thought, *Do deers' minds shut down?* and *Would mine shut down the same way?*

Shock makes your entire being collapse, no matter how you slice it. But don't humans know what to do, or do we, also, stand still? My guess is we'd react, but we'd hesitate too long.

My older brother was undeniably indecisive. So, I'd ask people, "A truck is bearing down on 'a kid,' but he knows there's a placid river on one side of the road. He also knows the reverse side has a 10,000-foot cliff. Which side does he choose?" The answer is obvious. Still, I chuckle and answer, "He gets hit by the truck!"

Given a deer's dismal outlook, exactly like my brother's, don't most of us get hit? Additionally, I wondered, "Do deer ignore their alternatives like our last-ditch philosophy, 'kiss yourself goodbye'?" If you did take the time to question all this, that's a lot to think about.

Unfortunately, one sunny day, I was forced to quickly think about that simultaneously as my life flashed right before my eyes.

I was pulling up to a stop sign across the street from my son's preschool. I was wistfully thinking about all the fun quality time we were going to have together. I also thought I was extremely blessed to have my little guy. And I naively thought we'd have so many more times together. Later, though, I realized I had been taking all those future times for granted.

At this same precise moment, I was forced (after a triple take) to glimpse a very fast car speeding right at me and not stopping! A ratty old battered Ford was barreling down on me right in the same intersection I was now halfway through. But I wasn't preoccupied with my driving; I was almost certain (like it really mattered) that I had the right of way. But there are situations that don't require being right. This was one of those times.

However, this other co-catastrophe person either didn't see his four-way stop sign or didn't care. Either way, his car continued to speed right at me. But then, it looked as if the driver was not even remotely thinking about stopping! Silly as it was, at that moment, all I could think was, *Oh, no.*

On cue, exactly like a startled deer, I froze, much to the chagrin of my earlier predictions. With my arms flailing in every direction, I screamed, "Holy moly!" At least, somewhere inside me, I also pontificated, *Some of my parts are reacting.* And my eyes were trying to somehow, magically, steer this oncoming car around me.

But my deerlike mind did absolutely nothing! Like deer in shock, all I could think was, *Brace yourself for impact* while I surmised, *I'm a goner.* Now, I have proof deer feel the same way I did. Wow! Who knew we each have the same immediate outlook and with no action either? And while I was primarily concentrating on being thoroughly mortified, this guy (or someone else) miraculously acted with blazing speed!

My intersection buddy must have finally realized what was happening, also. Then, everything seemed to happen in superslow motion:

At the very last instant, he systematically hit his brakes and slowed down his beat-up car enough to maneuver it around me within mere inches. Watching him go, literally, an angel's hair around my car was something I could not fathom. Only seconds before this, I was thinking, *I guess this is my time to go home!*

Immediately afterward, I sped through that intersection. Then, I stopped my car in the parking lot and sat there, shaking uncontrollably, for a solid hour! Obviously, I prayed a lot; I was also thanking my angel (my paternal grandmother, who is always with me). And I gave God a million thank-You(s)! All my thoughts were godly during that agonizing hour; I didn't understand who was responsible for altering that deadly course.

I thought my fellow driver seriously wanted us both dead! Then, he even vanished. The only troubled explanation I guessed was, "This was an act of God." And instead of taking me out of this world, God chose to share an epiphany with me of surely meeting Him at death's door.

But instead of ending my earthly life, He chose to educate me about my choices! Interestingly, a band I heard once said, "Even when you do nothing, you still have made a choice!" What did I not choose to do, Lord? But I already knew!

I believe, in crystal-clear terms, God told me, "This is not your time!" But He also sincerely impressed, "You're not doing anything for your brethren and Me." He intentionally forecast, "When you least expect it, your time on the earth can be over, and I will take you out of this earthly realm!" God was placing me on notice; He warned me, "Know your time here is finite," and, most importantly, "Do you know I am the one in control?"

Talk about someone with the greatest power, getting my attention and my priorities in order blazingly fast! They were certainly straightened out then.

For once, I felt truly convicted; even though I knew my purpose, I was proud and had been wasting my limited time, hoping for clarity. Right then, God handed me overwhelming eyes to see my life is very important; He stringently persuaded me, "Start now with your very specific passions and apply all your God-given gifts to accomplish your unique purpose."

Every week I still look forward to spending great times with my beautiful son, still driving through the intersection. Now, thank God, I always look both ways. But I also always look up! I'm also more appreciative of every day with my son. Now, though, I do it knowing this could be my last day cause all our days are numbered.

What's most important is what we do with our precious limited lives and who we do it for! I thank God every day, and I'm also trying to be productive with my time, helping others every chance I get. Saying it is one thing; doing it with our free will is something entirely different.

We're all born uniquely qualified for our one purpose: to resolve one human problem in the earthly realm. And every day, I must choose to fulfill my purpose because He has already forgiven my sins and saved me for my gloriously eternal tomorrows! He's only concerned now with my works. From birth, I've been given so many chances to make better choices and stop wasting God's gifts with my precious limited time.

Unlike so many unfortunate deer, my traumatic incident was a wake-up call to act! Maybe deer think, *What can I do?* But they still usually get hit.

Deer usually don't have choices. We do! Let His will be done with our choices.

LOUIE'S OMEN

In 2003, a close friend mentioned going to Louie's Restaurant, "It's a nice place to have a great time." He was attempting to coax me out of my apartment and funk for what seemed like eons. Likewise, I agreed to meet him there.

When I mentioned Louie's to another friend, he said, "It's a big Checker Motors hangout. But it's a great place to chill, have some great food, and laugh."

It was east of downtown, so I had never been there before. But I looked forward to Friday night's party. And once we got together, I was glad to discover Louie's really rocked! Surprisingly, it was jam-packed before 8 p.m.

They had a very entertaining, cool, three-piece band featuring a sultry-sounding woman vocalist who bragged she sang three decades worth of top hits. While she walked around the whole place, she sang songs people chose from their menus. She was a phenomenally talented singer and successful in getting everyone whipped up into a raucously loud frenzy!

The two other guys in the band were excellent musicians, and people were invited to sing with the band. But only *if* they knew the songs. A lot of people took advantage of the very different karaoke format with a live band backing them up, and it was a total blast. We had such a great time all night. But just as quickly, we learned the hoopla stopped when the clock turned 10 p.m. Talk about early nights? Who knew such a great time could happen in three very short hours?

My main problem was that night wasn't about fooling around; I had been having loads of playtime for way too long after, unfortunately, being prematurely unemployed. Obviously, bills piled up, and my creditors were bangin' down the door and calling me all the time. It was not kosher or fun.

Being in a deep depressive state was an understatement for my continuous, lousy situation. Regardless, I still knew to ask for what I needed and stay obedient. So, most nights, I prayed, "God, I really need some help. Could You help me with a new job yesterday?" I knew I was panicking and pushing Him; frustrated, I knew it would only happen in His time.

Once I heard a friend say, "God will not help desperate people" (or maybe it was "impatient" people). Either way, time was certainly against me. But what else could I do but follow Him? And He hadn't ever forsaken me. Nor would

He! This was about me needing to do what I could and having real faith; the fake stuff never quite works anyway. And why would it?

After that great Friday night, I decided to register with a few more temporary services. Nothing was coming my way, so I had to keep trying something. They normally did not have full-time work, but at least I'd have some money. Even though it would not pay all my bills, a wise, old friend once advised me, "Nine bucks an hour is way better than zero bucks." And if I worked hard, I could possibly be hired in after two or three months. Wow. *Hired*. That suddenly sounded hopeful.

With all that looming, I registered with a few local agencies. Amazingly, just one day later, OnStaff Temporaries called me and enthusiastically told me, "A client of ours was so impressed by your resume he would love to interview you tomorrow! Is that okay?"

I immediately asked her, excited about doing anything, "When can I start?"

She told me, "You have an interview with their president tomorrow. So, knock 'em dead!"

Luckily, the next day came, and a very fortunate thing happened: they loved my experience and said the four magic words any eager, unemployed-for-way-too-long person wants to desperately hear: "When can you start?"

I emphatically told them, "Today." But I started the next Monday.

When I left the interview, I thought, *Whew-wee! That was just in time, Lord!* I immediately looked toward heaven and let God know a heartfelt thank-You. Then I, sarcastically, added, "Great timing. You know I was scared to death?" I also thought, *What's the ol' saying? God only gives you what you can handle exactly when you need it?* So, off I went to my new job.

A friend gave me directions there, and I was driving east, on North Street, when I had this very weird sensation rush over me; for some strange reason, I suddenly turned to my right, and there was Louie's! What? Louie's? It was right down the street from where I needed to turn and go to my new employer's location!

It was totally unexpected, and as I laughed out loud, it felt as if I was being transported back into an old episode of *The Twilight Zone*. But everything was in color. This whole extended episode was sci-fi, bizarre, to me. Then, exactly like the first time, I looked up to heaven and asked Him, "Hey! Wazzup, God? What are You telling me right now?"

All I knew: even though I was seriously worried about my situation, I did three necessary for me things: I gave myself a break with a fabulous, stress-free night at Louie's; I let my friends care for me, and I asked God what I needed in a very serious prayer. I prayed for what I really needed. Most importantly, I had faith and trusted He would help me in His time!

Without even my knowing it, His miraculous plan was set in motion that Friday night on a very special corner in Kalamazoo, MI. Regardless, I wouldn't realize its significance until a few days after I started my new job.

But primarily, nothing would have happened if I didn't do something, and I prayed to God for what I absolutely needed the most, something He already knew. That has always been confusing for me; I needed to ask Him something He already knows. Guess that's the mysterious part about trusting Him; He couldn't give me what I needed, so I would never receive anything from Him without trusting Him first. Most believers call that *faith*.

I wholeheartedly believe there's an unspoken, supernatural agreement between God and you the instant you claim you are going to do something; He requires that from you! And I believe God is waiting for you to make an honest-to-goodness effort, even if it's a mental nod to

Him. He needs you to do your part, knowing you trust He can do His part.

Once, recently, our pastor dared everyone to double our tithes. The second I decided I would double my tithes, God was already working for my good. The next weekend I told my pastor, "I haven't received any blessings yet," thinking something would have happened already. It wasn't until the next day I was showered with blessings day after day after day.

One of them was nearly a $2-an-hour raise and over $1,000 back pay. Praise God because before I learned I was getting a pay raise, my increased tithe agreement with God was already in effect! God had already afforded my extra giving months earlier and kept His participation hidden.

Louie's was my catalyst; Louie's was my omen, and Louie's helped me receive God's saving grace exactly when I needed it most. Thank you, Louie's, and thank You, O merciful God! I needed Your help at my dire hour, and You were there for me. Thank You for another lesson!

BROWN CRAYONS

Brianna sat with her head hanging low in her pink-colored bedroom. Her soft curly locks fell all around her darling face. But her damp blouse made it painfully clear her tears had been falling over an excruciatingly long time. Her dilemma: every inch of her three-foot-five-inch tall, scrawny frame loved the Yoo-hoo chocolate milk. "But today," she cried, "there's no Yoo-hoo!"

Brianna loved everything about Yoo-hoo! Every time her mama poured the cool concoction into her glass, the smell tantalized her. Looking at it amazed her. She admitted, "It looks like a slippery chocolatey shake." Even hearing it splashing down into the bottom of her glass sounded yummy. Still, her very favorite part was tasting its "delishshuness"!

She happily thought, *It's heavenly*, and swirled it around in her mouth, creating a maximum mocha explosion of pleasure. Brianna's blue eyes brightened every time she guzzled down the oozing brown liquid.

Today, however, Brianna sat crushed. Her mommy forgot her Yoo-hoo! More tears fell, and she wondered, "Doesn't she love me anymore? How could she be so insensitive?"

She felt terribly tortured because, after pleading with Mama, "Didn't you get any Yoo-hoo?" her mommy said, "Sorry, precious. They were out today."

Her daddy also looked at Brianna's pouty face and said, "Sorry, sweetie." It didn't help.

So, knowing she didn't have a chance, she begged him, "Daddy, can you get some? Mommy didn't get any Yoo-hoo today!"

He shook his head and, sympathetically, promised Brianna, "We'll get some tomorrow, honey."

But Brianna was utterly crushed. Her single ponytail bounced around her head, and she stuttered, "To-mor-row is far away, Daddy!" and stormed toward Tommy's room. However, without knowing, her "meany" brother was waiting for her. He was smiling because he, too, knew Brianna loved Yoo-hoo.

Masking a big, fat, teasing grin, he said, "I have some mocha for you, Sissy." Momentarily, her long eyelashes bugged open. But immediately, she spotted the huge smirk on his hawkish face and realized, much too late, that he was also tormenting her. And as unbearable pain coursed through her tiny frame (without Yoo-hoo), she managed to blurt out, "How much more can a little girl take?"

Never-ending tears fell down her puffy cheeks as Tommy's taunting laughter pierced her heart. Brianna's mom yelled at Tommy, but he had already inflicted more phenomenal pain. Still, Tommy shouted in a feisty manner, "Mom, she's just a big baby; it's just chocolate milk! Whaaaa!"

That was when Brianna bolted into her room and slammed the door. But it was, coincidentally, the same time her favorite grandfather, PaPa, appeared.

PaPa eased Brianna's door open, saw her fuchsia-colored sundress spewed all around her spindly lily-white legs, and soothingly asked her, "What's wrong, baby girl?"

Her limp body was nestled in his lap before he knew it, and she whimpered, "PaPa, there's no Yoo-hoo today. And Tommy's been so mean to me!"

PaPa felt her whole body trembling while he listened intensely to her recounting of the daylong misery.

Afterward, he simply asked her, "Sweetie, d'ya have any brown crayons?"

Her silky brown bangs hung over a quizzical stare, and she muttered, "PaPa, why brown crayons?"

The mystery continued as PaPa repeated, "Do you have any brown crayons, baby?"

She answered, "Yes." But she was baffled and asked him, "Why do you need brown crayons, PaPa?"

Her first stumper was followed by, "What has that to do with my Yoo-hoo?" PaPa laughed at the barrage of questions, and his gentle eyes smiled back at Brianna wearing her "I'm Grandpa's cutie-pie" sundress.

The fact was that, unbeknownst to Brianna, PaPa secretly brought a big cold glass of white milk with him and some very cool Yoo-hoo into the den right next to her bedroom. He called the house earlier to, unfortunately, discover Brianna's extremely traumatizing news. He also knew very well Yoo-hoo is Brianna's favorite. And he came over to rescue her!

But instead of showing Brianna the Yoo-hoo right away, he came in with a glass of white milk. Momentarily, hoping upon hope it was her Yoo-hoo, Brianna let out another huge sigh, seeing, "It's only milk!"

Even with her pitifully sad face, PaPa repeated, "Do you have any brown crayons, kiddo?"

That was when Brianna's frustrated shoulders drooped over; this continuous agony furthered her family's horrible games, and she silently mused, *Now, even PaPa's being cruel to me.*

With a very long "Heeeeeere," and still feeling very traumatized, Brianna gave her PaPa her best brown crayon. Then, still very much upset, she wondered, "Why do you need stupid brown crayons anyway?"

He whispered, "Just close those dreamy eyes of yours, sweetie, and I'll be right back with a very tasty treat."

Brianna tightly squeezed her eyes and prayed, "God, pleeeeeeze, make it Yoooooo-hoooooooo!" Her mama always told her, "Pray really hard to God, Brianna, if you want something that bad."

After what seemed like an eternity, PaPa returned, and Brianna's blue eyes exploded open as she bolted for PaPa. She confidently thought, *That ooey-gooey surprise is my dream come true!* In Papa's right hand, thankfully, was a tall cold glass of yummier-than-all-get-out Yoo-hoo in her favorite Goofy-labeled glass! "Yay," she shouted out and pounced on her even-more favorite PaPa.

She simultaneously licked her lips, retrieved the chocolatey potion, and drank it down as quickly as she could, immediately filling her whole insides with that magical elixir. That was followed by a huge Cheshire grin on her deliriously happy face, and her whole body felt magnificent. Her face beamed complete bliss, and her dazzling eyes exhibited adoring love for her PaPa! And once it was gone, Brianna hugged PaPa very tightly.

Then, PaPa felt a million butterfly kisses flutter over his whiskered face, and she whispered, "I love you so much, PaPa!" PaPa also loved her that much, and her smile melted his heart as a single tear eased down his weathered cheek. The simple truth was Brianna loved Yoo-hoo as much as PaPa loved her!

He knew, "You and me, kid. We can't be happier?"

But then Brianna became stealthily quiet, looking his way and wondering as it was almost hitting her, "PaPa, how d'ya actually turn the plain, white milk into Yoo-hoo?"

PaPa knew his smart granddaughter would, eventually, realize his clever ruse. On cue, he admitted, "I put your brown crayon between my hands, coloring end toward the milk. Then, lightning-fast, I spun it between my palms until the brown crayon got fiery hot. Then, the volcano-hot crayon started dripping chocolatey magical syrup right into your milk." That's when PaPa smirked and said, "It was that easy."

Brianna was stupefied and only half believed PaPa's story. Then, she wryly smiled as a wide-eyed look surfaced on her pudgy face, and it made PaPa chuckle. Even her long eyelashes didn't stop fluttering. Still confused, she keenly asked PaPa, "What?"

Without missing a beat, her gentle PaPa asked her, "Hey, sweetness, do you also like strawberry-flavored milk?"

"Sure, PaPa," she spoke softly. "Strawberry's yummy. But it's not as dee-lec-ta-ble as Yoo-hoo!"

PaPa agreed, "I think strawberry Yoo-hoo isn't even half as dee-lis-shus as chocola-tey Yoo-hoo! Absolutely correct, my dearest."

But there still was some sneakiness on PaPa's endearing face. Attempting to half hide a sheepish grin, he gazed deeply into his only granddaughter's beautiful blue eyes and slowly asked her, "Brianna, do you have any red crayons?" She hesitated. But then, she got it! Acknowledging his wayward hint, she smiled and marched down with him into the kitchen with two small red crayons!

Standing in the kitchen, PaPa winked at his giddy accomplice because Brianna couldn't stop giggling. All of a sudden, she blurted out, "Mommy, is there any milk left?"

Then, she winked at PaPa and asked her mama, "PaPa and I are gonna make some strawberry milk! Okay?"

Her mama turned to her sneaky-looking dad and wondered, "What're you two doin', Mr. Funny Man?"

Then, she quizzically looked straight at Brianna and said, "What?"

WHAT REALLY MATTERS

I appreciate things now more than ever. And I believe true appreciation only comes with age. When my parents split up, my father told me, "I'll always love your mom. But I can't live with her anymore." It confused me because I thought, *How could you truly love Mom but cannot live with her?* He taught me, "There are all kinds of love." And living with someone is never easy and certainly more stressful when it's not good!

Much, much later, my future ex-wife helped me fully realize estrangement as I, tearfully, left the only house I ever owned. Also, after that catastrophic phase of my life, I was able to discern things in a much different light. One thing was once having a nice collection of trinkets (something I learned to be practical about and create over time):

In 1989, my wife and I visited our friend's house. They had a sizeable collection of German Hummels. But I grew up without a lot of nice things, so I was, selfishly, very materialistic. Naturally, I was extremely envious of our friend's beautiful collectibles; their collection made me wonder when we'd start having a comparable one.

And even though I quickly wanted lots of pieces, my

wife was more practical. She said, "They're very expensive, so if we get 'em one at a time, we'll have a nice considerable set sooner than you think." Luckily, she was right. But then I didn't appreciate why it was very important to consciously celebrate each moment of our collection!

My wife and I decided we really enjoyed Precious Moments figurines and Swarovski crystals. We loved them and, over many life events (holidays, birthdays, anniversaries), continued collecting one piece at a time. Eventually, those pristine collections grew, and I thought I thoroughly enjoyed each moment surrounding each gift (or did I?).

When we moved into our first home, I bought my wife a Precious Moments. The polished porcelain figurine depicted a boy and a girl building a sandcastle house by hand. It easily described us making our house a very lovely home.

Also, in 1995, we brought our sheltie puppy, Jenni, home. Because of that special occasion, I gave my wife another Precious Moments; it was a little boy sitting on a stoop and eating a chocolate-chip ice-cream cone and dripping it all over. Anxiously waiting for her licks beside the little boy was his ever faithful, always hungry, nearly patient puppy.

Even more strange—our puppy figurine also elicited an amazing premonition. When we brought Jenni home, we had mostly accepted we weren't going to have children. But we always wanted them and thought it would be very special to have them. We knew it was a bitter pill to swallow. Still, a pregnant coworker of mine once warmly advised me, "Get a puppy and love it to death. Then, God will see you can love something else unconditionally." I guess it was shockingly true because...

Surprisingly, in May 1998, our baby boy's birth was our most miraculous, overdue, and very welcome collectible! And we couldn't be more overjoyed. When it finally dawned on me, I realized the boy figurine was forecasting our destiny: an ice-cream boy and his hungry girl puppy!

When we brought our son home, I gave my wife another Precious Moments. She absolutely loved the porcelain piece that portrayed a small swaddled infant lying in his carriage. We both were supremely happy, and I fondly remember the tears flying down my wife's pretty face. The day we both, secretly, wanted for so very long, but never thought would happen, most certainly came!

Consequently, as seventeen years of special occasions passed, our collections blossomed. One day friends swung by, and I saw myself in them when their faces lit up, seeing such a beautiful collection sitting in lighted curios. It made me remember how amazed I was by our friend's cute pieces. That day I truly appreciated how wonderfully they accented our home. But something else, strangely, happened.

Even though I admired every piece, my memories shifted to the moments behind each treasured piece. A big, fat grin covered my face when I appreciated the special time I gave my fiancée her very first Precious Moments. It was a young boy and his girlfriend giggling at each other on opposite sides of an old maple tree with their names carved inside a huge heart. It was one of the happiest days of our lives! But much later, we embarked on a bitter breakup.

Unfortunately, our judgment of divorce legally decreed our collectibles were not *our* collection; they were legally considered *gifted* to my wife, and that's how they were distributed. I was understandably sad and felt the court, unsympathetically, stipulated I was never actually part of all our memories. What anyone else thought didn't matter to me; I gave all of them with my heart!

Strangely enough, losing literally everything helped me see those precious gotta-have-them-now possessions could never give me the kinda joy I've always wanted. Even though they were very nice to look at, without each one's attached sentimentality, it's all they'd ever be. Nowadays, possessions can't make me happy, and they certainly are not what I need.

I believe real happiness is a by-product of attaining what you want out of life (your goals), and people are always unduly confused. All I ever hear is, "I just wanna be happy!" Although, coincidentally, what they really desire is to do what they want (for example, a satisfying career). Likewise, once they're in their dream job, their inevitable by-product is the happiness they were searching for!

Realistically, nice collections are extremely special. But you really have nothing but them if your energy isn't laser-focused on treasuring and nurturing the very substantial yet fragile relationships they're based upon. Basically, we need to appreciate every moment while we're *in* it! It may seem difficult, but it's totally necessary.

Unfortunately, I discovered that painfully hardest lesson way too late. And it took me almost four years to recover. But I humbly learned that without a cherished love within a solid relationship, your precious things are, simply, novelties adorning loveless homes. Without that sustaining magic, your collectibles really don't mean a thing; the sentimentality, realistically, fades, and they're forever tainted! I haven't seen one of those pieces in over twenty years, and I really don't want to.

Nowadays, what I appreciate most is that I do not need to have nice things around me and that they're no big deal! My life is much happier because I now fully grasp a much more liberating concept. I was finally blessed to learn life goes on easily without collectibles and with little hardship. Those pieces had emotional value. But valuing intangibles is more relevant!

After dealing with a troubling split, I garnered one monumentally special piece of clarity; I was finally able to focus on the important parts of my life; I learned to embrace relationships, have loving friendships, and treasure every precious moment I have with my fun-loving, handsome son.

Initially, it was extremely hard to lose everything that I thought mattered. Philosophically, one beautiful tree is all you see (and want), but you, stubbornly, miss the whole forest, and it disappears around you. Luckily, I was eventually able to fully appreciate my family, my friends, Jenni's infrequent visits, and my always adorably cute son. I know they're what really matters!

They are my most treasured collections. So, I had to streamline my life to demonstrate to them and me that they're my highest priority! I fully appreciate every minute we're together because I, thoughtfully, focus on enjoying every moment. And lighted curios aren't necessary! The truth is no batteries or electricity are required; they, naturally, light up my life.

Every day, we should shine our light on everyone. Being collected is always nice, too; it means they want to be around you, and that's their biggest compliment.

MY FATHER'S KISS

He kissed me. My father kissed me right smack on the lips in front of a zillion people. I shrank when he came at me because I was embarrassed. I asked myself, *Why did he do that? Two grown men don't kiss like that in front of others, especially!*

What reason do parents have to do these things to their kids? Even then, kids remember the most insignificant things parents do for them. Moms and Dads vehemently try to ensure their kids not only have great things but greater times! So, they buy them cars, take them on trips, or get them that one favorite toy every year. I believe they do it out of love, but I also believe their biggest hope is two things: (1) their provision will guarantee their baby's childhood has great memories, and (2) their children will grow up happy kids.

Contrary to their good wishes, many years later, parents realize something else is their child's best memory. It wasn't that pony. And it was not your family visit to the baseball stadium.

The smallest act by Mommy or Daddy is what their child remembers. Maybe it was how big that stadium was, and "how Daddy protected me when I was scared." It could also be that hug you gave them at a vulnerable moment; that one magical act sealed their memory. And it was all about the intensity of the moment for them! Things may seem important, but cherished memories are what children need to remember.

I have many magnificent memories with my *daddy*. But one memory sticks out; it was a beautiful day covered with a crystal-clear blue sky. I was twenty-three years old, and my dad and I were standing inside a terminal at Orange County's John Wayne International Airport. We were part of a huge crowd waiting to board our plane, and my dad came to say goodbye.

I've always been very close with my dad, and he's always been very affectionate with me. Like a million other times, I gave my dad a big, bear hug. I loved him and hated leaving him, but it was so much more about not knowing when I'd see him again. Then, without warning, my dad (for no godly reason) came at me, wanting to give me a kiss square on the lips. Ugh!

In seconds, he planted his affections on me! "Dad, what are you doing?" I wondered, and, "Why, Dad?" For what felt like an eternity, I felt shocked and embarrassed. During those moments, inside, I was screeching, *What are you doing to me, Dad, in front of all these people?* I was literally knocked for a loop because he'd never kissed me before like that. The simple fact was I couldn't fathom it, and I was so insecure.

When eternity ended, I semicontrolled my emotions and quickly admitted to everyone, "Hey, folks. My dad, apparently, really loves me, and he wanted to shower me with a big, loveable, I'm-not-embarrassed-by-any-of-this-are-you smooch. That's the show! Let's disperse now and get over it. Okay?"

I was thoroughly unaware of my dad's motivation that day, but I can remember a lot of great times with him.

When I remember our airport moment, my heart, mind, and soul seem to converge (or therapist-speak "convolute"), and it's super uncomfortable. I don't fully understand why it's bothering me so much! Then, my heart starts pumping faster and faster, and I'm wearing a huge smile.

The feelings go round and round, and now, I'm my father's son. Then, I'm a daddy, and my thoughts get hazy. It's clear I'm very happy no matter who I am. Whenever I remember my dad and me together, I'm suddenly my son's daddy, and those weird memories blend into happy times with him. Magically, it seems, all my father-and-son thoughts intermingle, and I'm brought back to fascinating memories between Owen and me. But I'm focused on how he makes me feel.

My times together with my son are nothing I've ever known (feelings-wise); it's the closest I've come to pure love. I've always felt so alive and wistful whenever I'm with him, and those loving feelings manifested into many, many hugs and I-love-you(s). It's all about how he makes me feel and what he means to me!

I've "planted" a million kisses on him for no good reason other than wanting him to know how incredible he makes me feel. I smell his hair, kiss his head, and, again, I'm amazed at how beautiful he is. No obligation. Just action. He makes me feel silly, and I continuously say, "I love you," and, "You make Daddy so happy." Because he makes me feel ecstatic, my feelings seem to elicit a reaction. And I suppose my affections are for him and me.

I've staunchly learned when you're in love, you unconditionally give your whole self to that person; you need them to know how lucky you are that they're in your life. I truly can't remember my life without my son. He helped me relearn that love is precious when it's given voluntarily; you instinctively do things you know they like, and thankfully, that also makes you happy. I'm thankful for every great memory, and I always want more and more fun times.

Like most parents', my refrigerator is plastered with crazy pictures of us together. My favorite picture is of a two-month-old Owen and me lying down for a nap. We were lying at the bottom of the bed and could not get any closer. The proximity explains when we're together, I genuinely don't know where I end and he starts. Every time I think about that nap, I smile. I only wanted to be there and close to him. I was his protector and felt so much love for my miracle boy. Who knew a nap was so refreshing and life-altering?

When I see that photo, I feel that intense joy for Owen again. I'm also amazed at how suddenly babies go to sleep; babies go forever until there's no more "go." Then, sleep is instantaneous.

I believe babies have an innate sense of being loved and protected; the security blanket creates a comfort level and enables babies to drift off. I call it "innocent sleep." It's also a great thing to witness up closely and personally.

While I was lying there, nothing else mattered. And sleep was inevitable; I was warm, I loved my little boy dearly, and, most of the time, I was exhausted! Daddies need naps, too.

Another picture is: Owen and I in front of a big old-fashioned train called "The Logger" (Yosemite National Park). Owen was sitting on my shoulders and softly wiggling my ears. It's something neat he's done since he was a baby; we'd lie in his bed after story time. Then, he'd wiggle my ears and drift off; it was our connection. He felt connected to his daddy and was, finally, comfortable visiting Sleepyland.

That picture shows our tired smiles, how I held his feet so he wasn't scared, and, again, how I didn't know where I stopped and he started. We've always been connected; we always have fun, and we, honestly, love being together! What can be better?

After soccer practice, the next day, my son, his grand-father, and I were involved in an unplanned water-hose "fight." My son surprised us with Dad's garden hose. Moreover, my dad and I were completely drenched. Then, laughing, my dad asked me, "Wha' d'ya think would happen when he grabbed that hose?"

"In a way, I hoped it would happen," I said. The best thing about it was my mom was taking pictures of her "three drenched rats."

The picture captured the overall essence of our little family. The wackiest thing I see is Owen, hose-ready and laughing his fool head off. I couldn't be happier because this time together was magical; after four years, I was delighted to finally have my paternal family together. I called it "completing a father, son, and grandson circle of life." Mindlessly, I didn't know if I was still the father or the son (and getting drenched was silly and a huge bonus).

Another favorite photograph from the fall recently landed on my refrigerator. We were at my girlfriend's house, and, unbeknownst to me, Owen was helping her rake leaves. Then, my goofball son wanted her to bury him in that mound of multicolored leaves. Oh, my!

Other than those mounds of leaves, all I see is his cute little face poking out in the middle! I shake my head and mutter, "What a goober." And another smile lands on my face. That's when I realize he's a lot like his daddy; he's an affable nut, and we have the same crazy tendencies. My boy loves to laugh (the sillier, the better), and I'm a part of our insanity. And I see me in him.

But the most remarkable thing I notice is Owen is the happiest boy I've ever known! Any reason to laugh and play—he's right in the thick of it. Dozens of pictures portray his beaming, goofy smile, and he's the biggest joy in my life.

We have so much fun together, and I'm extremely blessed he loves me. It means so much, and he has also brought out the best sides of me. Fortunately, I love to share every one of them with him.

Much of his personality comes from growing up completely adored and showered with tons of incredible affection. Plus, he's taken full advantage of the loving environment we created! One joke we had was, "What's your full name?" and he'd answer, cute as a button, "Ding-a-ling." Cute. All those pictures bring back so many slapstick memories, and I truly can't stop smiling; they all make me so happy!

Remembering all those crazy times suddenly shook me like an earthquake's seismic waves shifting the earth's plates; in my innermost consciousness, all those cumulative memories spun around and pushed my mind toward a shocking epiphany. Simultaneously, when all those great memories washed over me, I realized why my father kissed me that glorious day!

As I was leaving California, my dad was having all those same feelings for me! He had also witnessed his most treasured pictures and remembered all our times together. He had the same love for me, and he wanted to passionately show me how much he still loved me. So, without hesitation, his heart and mind told him, "Kiss him now!" And, thankfully, he did!

Tossing back and forth from "Owen's daddy" to "my dad's son" made me remember things from my childhood when I was his little boy.

When I was very young, I always knew how much my dad loved me; it was in every word and action, and I completely adored my dad. Sometimes I wondered if my heart would burst from loving him so much. I now know (thank God) that the same love I continuously shower on my son comes directly from the love my daddy showered on me! It's generational.

When I was growing up, my father was my primary motivator and a very active cheerleader. I can't describe how great I felt and how extremely confident and loved I was because I knew I was very special to him. In his eyes, I could do anything, and he often said, "You really can do anything in this world, Jimmy." Most times, I felt ordinary. But my dad always made me feel as if my "achievements" were phenomenal.

Many times I questioned, "Why, Dad?" But it didn't matter; he believed it, and that made me feel special, knowing it was always straight from his heart. And, no matter what I did, he always made it sound as if I was an exceptionally gifted athlete, student, etc. But time helped me realize I really needed that and so does Owen! Maybe, in our own way, all fathers are trying to give their kids that kinda love.

At the airport, I didn't appreciate the intensity of my dad's love; I was nowhere close to understanding his specific kinda love until I was blessed with my own beautiful boy. And until then (to love and kiss a billion times), I couldn't know the depths of my dad's love for me. Until nearly nine years ago, I was utterly clueless about the bliss my dad felt for me all my life, but especially on that gorgeous Californian day. Thankfully, now, I realize how it feels to be in love with my son—exactly as my dad felt that day at the airport!

Naively, back then, I didn't know how much he felt for me. With all the enormous love bubbling up inside of him (like whenever I hold Owen), my father acted the way all those emotions forced him to do. My father kissed me! In a huge crowd, maybe he kissed me to openly demonstrate how much he loved me. But I, undoubtedly, believe he had to kiss me!

Immaturely, I was mortified, and my naivete caused a wave of complete embarrassment. Despite that, now, I believe I'm the only one who felt bad then; I believe all those people around us probably felt my father's kiss was sweet. I was the only one overreacting! His kiss was beautiful, but throughout my entire life, he gave me so many more wonderful gifts.

When I was very young, my father excessively made it clear, "You should go out and make your memories. You certainly won't make any sitting here." "Then," he'd say, "you'll have lotsa interesting stories to tell people."

As a former long-haul trucker of vast experience, he advised me, "Drive out West and have your car break down in the middle of nowhere." The concept was ludicrous, but it also made me burst out laughing. However, my dad was not kidding! He'd also philosophically repeat his "it's the journey, not the destination" mantra. I was also supposed to keep on truckin', but that was a great credo. And once, I did break down, "out west."

Outside Albuquerque, one ominous-looking afternoon, near dusk, my Renault Alliance started sounding weird. All I heard was my dad repeating, "You should always listen to weird sounds emitting from your car." Sarcastically, I only have fond memories of lifting my car's hood while the summer sun sank behind a huge hill.

I hovered over the engine, shivering, as a fierce chilly wind blew icy tendrils down the back of my short-sleeved shirt. Dad was also my Boy Scout troop leader. He warned us, "Be prepared for changing weather out West." That was when I nearly strangled myself with my scarf; it was dangerously hanging down, right over the engine's running fan blade!

Perplexed, I thought, *What am I doing? I can't fix cars. My dad fixes cars!* Thankfully, I took all his advice. And I also collected hundreds of fun-filled, fantastic memories throughout my life. I was blessed to travel through fourteen European countries, Canada, Mexico, and forty-six states. But I keep a special memory close to my heart of my dad and me when I was twelve years old.

Despite the breathtaking Utah-mountain scenery displayed in front of us and the Herculean effort my dad persevered to get us up there, my memory's focused on a mental snapshot. It shows my dad and me sitting quietly on a solitary park bench and eating a late lunch. It was beautiful up there, and some large puffy clouds were pierced by the sun's rays.

Fortunately, a big part of my heart will always be right there with my daddy sitting on an old park bench and eating Stuckey's chicken. It's a major emotional time in my life!

Lunch was delicious, and I felt totally happy. I remember never wanting to be anywhere else, and I was certain I didn't want that moment to end! It was truly profound, and, in many respects, it never ends. My dad told me, "Anytime you want, you can see it crystalized in your mind's eye." And now, every time I see that scene, I cannot stop smiling and feel extremely happy. I'm full of immense joy, and warm feelings flood all over me until I'm shivering with those clammy goose bumps!

Then, again, it hits me: hey, those are the same feelings I have whenever I remember Owen and me together! I love my dad so much, and I'd like to think I love him more than he'll ever know. But I'd be very wrong; my daddy knows how much I love him: he proved how much he loved me that sensational day at the airport in front of zillions.

When we were at that mountainside bench, my dad and I created an everlasting memory. And exactly as he said about making my own memories, this is a very interesting story I can tell people. Dad loved me, and he generously gave me that magnificent photograph to keep in my mind's eye.

It's the same reason he wanted to give me that unforgettable kiss all those years ago! That was my dad; his actions were always unexpected, unconventional, and 150 percent authentic about everything he did. I always act real because of him. My father's kiss doesn't embarrass me anymore. I relish it! Miss you terribly, Daddy-O. Hope we can laugh again soon. I'll bring the Stuckey's chicken!

MY TESTIMONY

In the last twenty-five years, I was fired from about twenty-five jobs, including being fired from my last, good job on March 26, 21, where I worked very hard for five and a half years. And no matter why being fired isn't fun, it's definitely not a joke.

However, my last termination was different from all the others because I wasn't concerned about my immediate loss of income and benefits. I don't really know why, but I realized who caused me to feel secure in what should have been an emotionally wrecked storm; "It happened again," I said. But the tears didn't fall. I had become a different person, experienced at trauma, and I was made whole to cope with anything only with God's help.

I came to Mt. Zion Baptist Church in Kalamazoo, MI, in 2009. The church was on a long list of places where I could ask for "donations" to pay my back rent. Unfortunately, eviction was imminent; I was totally worried, and I had just totaled my new car. For Mt. Zion's donations, they required me to attend a Bible study, a fulfillment-hour class, and one sermon with a bonus breakfast. Already, without even knowing it, I was being groomed for a Mt. Zion membership!

I was greeted at the door by Pastor Moore (and un-knowingly blessed). But the person shaking my hand wasn't Dr. Addis Moore, and he didn't serve me breakfast either. But I quickly realized nothing happened at Mt. Zion without our pastor's blessing. Fortunately, I liked every-thing about my experience. And many, many people shook my hand that Sunday and let me know, "It was nice to see you today." That, too, was Pastor Moore's doing.

On the marquee outside the church, there's a mantra, "If you show up, you will grow up." It seemed quite mean-ingful, and it made me wonder, "Is this place good for me?" I should have known, "You finally arrived. Start the training." I liked it so much that I kept coming. How else would I grow up *if* I didn't show up?

Mt. Zion blessed me with a $300 donation, and I was never evicted! But this was just one of many lessons to-ward being obedient, and so I could expect many blessings (something else very uncommon to me).

I was raised to give without expecting anything. So, this was new and strange to me, especially being obedient. Once, I remember Pastor Moore reciting Scripture about doing all ten things on a list of ten. He said, "If you only do nine things, it's like you didn't do anything." This obedient thing was gonna be hard because I was a casual, not-so-serious kinda guy when it came to doing everything on any list. But I needed to try even though I once heard, "Trying is the first step toward losing; you've got to do something."

I was saved on November 19, 1981. Years later, I learned my Mt. Zion-designated disciple's birthday was November 19. How's that for a God thing? But I wasn't ever a "practicing Christian" (for nearly thirty years). Mt. Zion's school, however, was my first experience at practicing. One time I even stood up in church and vehemently declared, "Mt. Zion keeps me serious about Jesus." I felt very convicted by all my Mt. Zion experiences, including baptism!

Over the years, I attended many Bible studies, fulfillment classes, and hundreds of Pastor Moore's fiery sermons. From the back row, my very young son once asked me, "Why does he have to be so loud?"

I answered him, "I guess that's how he gets his very important message across to his flock." However, try telling that to a seven-year-old.

Either way, I continued attending. I had several ministries (required and necessary); I gave below my 10-percent tithe and continued to learn and practice. Mt. Zion has always been more assertive about teaching the Word, applying the Word in our lives, and ensuring all of Kalamazoo's unbelievers hear the good news!

Also, my Christian training taught me so many practical scriptures, and I learned about and felt close to being transformed by Christ alone. Ironically, transformation is akin to "showing up" and "growing up." Talk about deep, huh? And the only way to transform yourself is by pouring lots of Jesus Christ into you and recognizing the power that's inside you (with our Holy Spirit, another blessing).

Gracefully, all you are inside is like little Jesuses or Christians. I remember many years ago, kids ridiculed church kids (as if they were weird). Nowadays, my transformation at Mt. Zion left me declaring, "I don't care what anyone says about me. I love going to church, I love serving others, and I think it's weirder not going to church every Sunday." I also felt another great feeling—of being blessed. And my education enabled me to know what being blessed meant, and I was very glad to have His blessings.

Once, I heard Pastor Moore say, "You need Jesus!" But I never knew what that really meant; I just thought it was something Christians said to heathens like me. But I learned Christians who say that mean two important things: (1) Jesus is the only one who can save you, and (2) the only way to the Father is through His Son, Jesus.

Another thing I experienced is the folks saying that they honestly cared about me! The truth is: I found people not only need Jesus but also people who care enough about them to also let them know what they should be doing. They made me conscious of also being accountable to God and my brethren.

I'm not a Bible-scripture memorizer, but I've read the whole Bible a few times. So, I know many educational Bible stories through Dr. Moore. During his sermons, he repeatedly recited lots of verses. He said, "It's very important for you to speak Scripture all the time." But we were "fed" biblical nourishment from our intelligent pastor and swallowed his lessons whole (to enjoy its dessert). To me, that's transformational!

Many people have said, "You'll never be bored when Pastor Moore is ministering" (dancing included). That all those teachings unequivocally helped me is an enormous understatement; they saved me many times. But most importantly, they gave me a renewed inner peace I had never known. I was blessed to have a few disciples who honestly cared about me and wanted me to tell them my whole story so I would continue to transform happily.

My church experiences were extremely helpful. But even though I was being obedient, thinking I was improving my work life, I kept finding ways to get fired and re-hurt.

Each time, though, I strangely felt less hurt, knowing Jesus was alongside me. Recently, I heard a song called "He Knows." The moral is: He's been through any kind of pain I could imagine. My ol' way of thinking wasn't correct or even aligned with God's Word. My thoughts were always foggy, and I wasn't discerning things correctly, mainly because I still thought my thinking was right! That was a very troubling obstacle for me.

Also, my dad's lifelong lessons mixed me up, and I continued finding ways not to learn what he always wanted me to know. So, I began changing, little by little. I really listened to my disciple's advice and finally heard it. Maybe, I was finally growing up. My dad was still in my life but was too far away and an atheist raised as a Christian. Now a Jew.

When I told him what my disciple and I were working toward, he paused. Then, he said, "Jimmy, I've been saying those same things to you your whole life. Despite that, I'm glad your disciples are finally helping you find your way!" After sixty years, I was finally headed in God's only direction for me. To Him.

We had to work on that little thing I can't always see (or something I wasn't doing). Proudly, again, I knew I was right until it dawned on me how wrong I was all along. Once, I lost my job only three months after my son was born. It really hurt my entire family. And I lost another state job when I was angry at my wife for our divorce; I realized too late she had had enough and could not wait for me anymore to wise up (and grow up).

I told people my breakup pretty much cost me everything important. But it really hurt losing so many future times with my four-year-old son. I realized I had to change soon and finally grow up. That was 2001, and, unfortunately, it would be a long time before I matured and grew up.

It's now 2022 (many years later). Even though my growing up will never stop, I feel and think differently. I'm calm, a lot more patient, and so much more peaceful. I cope much better and know where to go with my issues; I pray to God (He asked), but I still naively wonder, "Doesn't He already know this?" I guess that's all part of "being obedient." Do I still have a crisis in my life? Definitely! We will always have trials and tribulations.

Good thing Pastor Moore's sermons were always full of warnings: "Count on it; Christians will have trials and tribulations!" And much of that same theology resurfaces when I need peace. So, I ask Him, and He gives me more peace. Even though I've learned many great things like forgiveness and "giving it all to God," I still don't fully practice that particular godly "art." Luckily there's room for improvement, more learning, and maturity.

My traumatic youth caused me to control everything. Though problematic, I could only give God 98.4 percent of my control because, as I once told a friend, "I don't know who I'd be if I gave Him *all* my control."

During many alter calls, I seriously gave Him all my worries. Afterward, though, I'd reach down and pick 'em up again (out of necessity). For nearly sixty years, I've felt I'm the only one who can fix me. Silly? Still, Jesus enabled me to see He was there for me my whole life. That was even before I was me, the person I was trying so desperately to save.

It had to be God who saved me from so many bad times and kept me going! I know God carried me when I neglected Him. But now, He's my proclaimed Refuge and Redeemer. Even after eleven years of Pastor Moore's training, I sadly confess God was not my first call during my next few crises; I still tried to, foolishly, handle things on my own. Funny thing: He let me.

God was my last call after another bout of "only Jim can save you." Talk about distracted free will. It was a lackluster reaction to another bad situation and me not handling it well. That's when I finally realized, "Why didn't I ask Him first?"

Toni, one of my dearest friends, once advised me, "When you take a leap of faith, God will either catch you or teach you to fly." I love that line; it was beautiful and timely news to me and made leaping easier! It was the "news flash" I ultimately needed.

One Sunday, after that realization, I gave Him all my control. The weirdest thing was I discovered turning me over was so much easier than I feared. God was always on my side, but He couldn't help me while my free will and I were standing in my naïve way. When helping myself didn't work (again), I realized I could be sitting in a deep, depressed state and trying to ponder a great way to escape from my latest hot mess. Turns out I was really depressed and not thinking; God taught me I didn't have any discerning powers!

I didn't fully trust how Mt. Zion equipped me to get myself through any situation. I hated, "You can't go under, over, or around it; you must go through it." Why? Because I knew if I skipped "going through it," I'd feel better. Like with anyone else, it hurt to feel so much pain from each additional tragedy. But I was about to learn I could either shabbily come up with another worst way to help myself or dare God. So, I shouted, "If You can do so much better than me, just do it!" I was scared to challenge Him, but I was also at my wits' end.

In my last two grave situations, He did exactly what I dared Him very successfully! When I let Him work all things out for my good, I humbly learned I would have never resolved my messes as He did; with His phenomenal resources, He picked one extraordinary way to reshape me 30,000 times healthier.

This last time, He was the one in control! It was a horrendous situation, but the Holy Spirit whispered, "Work on your lousy, hurt feelings and let God work it out for you in His time." It was all I really had the strength to do, and, like last time, I liked His way much better.

I felt a tremendous sense of peace; I knew God had this, and I was strangely confident everything would be resolved. The weird thing is how He did it, and I've never felt so completely cared for. Throughout this latest catastrophe, I should've been frantic. But I willingly gave it all to Him and was truly exhausted. I had reached my breaking point, but blessedly, I wasn't alone anymore; I had a great friend, confidante, and Savior!

Alone, I've fought many endless, defeated battles. I confessed, "Please, God? I need You because I can't handle all these heavy burdens anymore." And God pulled me through all of it (much better off). If I sat there, forever, faced with complete despair, I'd have never found His way to make it so much better.

Crisis 1,752: on March 26, 2021, I was fired again. But I never knew God had already decided I was not going to work there anymore. Rather quickly, I realized years of unbearable stress dripped off me. And strangely, my faith grew; losing my old job was His way of helping me, abruptly, move on. I did not even ask, "Where now, God?"

A friend once asked me, "How are you going to find out what your new life will be like unless you leave this one?"

During that next month, I should've constantly been looking for work, but I barely looked and was not worried. Again, thankfully, I finally 1,000 percent believed God would be taking care of me. I was even glad He was doing it. Then, in the middle of April, I halfheartedly answered a text for a contracted-driver job. I went to an interview at a local McDonald's and told the owner of the trucking company about my qualifications. And, *voila*! He hired me. I was shocked because that was way too easy. And my new boss is a Christian, also.

At my last job, I wasn't making enough, but we were an ESOP company (with a lucrative profit-sharing account my old company funded; probably an extra $7.00 an hour if I compared it with other employment offers). Happily, I started at my new, very secure trucking-company job (handling the US mail) at a 30 percent pay increase. And this company has an IRA ESOP, too (giving me an extra $3.11 an hour).

Obviously, I'm better off; only a year later, I'm making a lot more. I declare God placed me in a much happier life! And many great things continue to happen as I strive to be obedient. It may sound hard, but it's actually very easy (with continuous training).

I believe God did everything for me: He gave me time to remedy myself, He de-stressed my life, making it much calmer. I can also thank Him for a very flexible schedule that enables me to work elsewhere. I couldn't do any of this without God's reliable, constant help!

So, the greatest news about my experiences, before and after I gave it to God, is a message to everyone. Instead of looking at those monstrous dilemmas you must pass through, now:

1. Give it all to God first!

2. If you haven't done it already, please, give yourself to Jesus and the Holy Spirit. Right now, take your leap of faith. Don't think. Just say, "I trust You, Lord, with my whole messed-up life. I can't do this without You."

3. Most importantly, believe God (even dare Him just once). Ask Him to transport you into your new life, in a much better situation, where you can survive peacefully. Don't you desperately want that for yourself? Don't you want peace and not to fight anymore? It only takes a little trust, or a dare, for Him to change everything about your new life for good!

You must really believe this with all your heart. Ask yourself, "Have I ever done any better on my own?" Trust He will do that for you.

Note (the key): passing through all your pain is all you can do.

Practically, going through all that mess is all you can handle, and that's plenty. Only process through your hurting and trust He'll do the rest (and much, much more). If you completely believe and let Him go to work, He'll put you back on solid ground. He'll be your rock. But believing in Him is your key!

My hope is you'll make a godly choice and be in a much more peaceful place forever. It really takes complete faith and your effort. And it really does ask you to believe He is your victory.

I continue growing up, being fed by the Word, and meditating on it day and night. I know most Bible stories, but I can't tell you which chapter and verse they're from. I do know not to lean on my own understanding, so I must lean only on Christ.

Thank You, Jesus, for training us up in the way we should go (Proverbs 22:6).